# Bibliography, Historical and Bibliothecal

## *A Handbook of Terms and Names*

Philip H. Vitale
*Professor of English, De Paul University*

LOYOLA UNIVERSITY PRESS
Chicago   60657

Part I, page 3

Part II, page 169

© 1971 Loyola University Press
Library of Congress Catalog Card Number: 76-161657
ISBN 0-8294-0206-3
Printed and bound in the United States of America

# Preface

Bibliography, Historical and Bibliothecal aims to make readily available to the English major generally, and to the student of bibliography and research specifically, an identification of those terms and persons that relate significantly to the history of writing, printing, and publishing; to the development of libraries and to the systems of classification which govern the storage of written and printed works in them; and to the concepts of theory and practice which make for the most fruitful use of the works themselves.

There are a number of handbooks or manuals available which deal with the enumerative phase of bibliography, with the basic tools of research, the reference works themselves. And there are many works which deal with highly limited aspects of the historical or bibliothecal phases of bibliography, such as the history of the ancient library, the medieval library, the national libraries, the famous non-national libraries, the individual library (the Bodleian, the Cambridge University Library, the British Museum Library, the Library of Congress); or works which are concerned with, say, the history of writing, the making of paper by hand, bookbinding and the care of books, the development of type designs. But there is not, to my knowledge, a manual or handbook which highlights salient historical and bibliothecal data generally.

The arrangement throughout is alphabetical: in Part I, of the terms themselves; in Part II, of the names of those persons who have contributed significantly to the development of writing, printing, publishing, book collecting, and library growth. At times groups of cognate terms are combined under a single entry (e.g., paper, varieties of). Cross references are kept to a minimum.

iii

# Terms in the History of Writing, Printing, Publishing, Book Collecting, Book Selling, and Library Development

# A

**abbreviations**
 A writing method which was characteristic of medieval writers and carried over to some extent, especially in Latin, throughout the sixteenth century.

**acrophony**
 The use of a symbol to represent phonetically the initial sound (syllable or letter) only of the name of the object, of which it was previously the pictorial sign or hieroglyph. Thus, in the development of writing, the picture of the owl is first used as an ideogram to signify the bird itself, then as a phonogram to represent its name (Coptic moulaj), and finally, variously modified, it is employed to denote simply the initial sound m. The character beth, originally representing a house, is later used to indicate the sound of b, the initial of the word. In brief, then, it is the principle by which the symbol comes to stand for the initial sound of the word, rather than for the whole word.

**added entries**
 Entries which refer to a part of the whole, that is, to a bibliographical entity, such as the parts of a collective or serial work, of a single publication, in one or more volumes, with separate titles; chapters in books; articles in periodicals.

addendum
> A supplement to a book, especially a short supplement printed as a part of the book; also, one entry in such a supplement. Such a supplement (explanations, comments, additional items) is sometimes called an <u>addenda</u>.

advance copies
> Complete books (usually about a dozen) made up from the dummy copy as sales material or proof copies.

adversaria
> A miscellaneous collection of notes, remarks, or selections; a commonplace book; also, commentaries or notes, as on a text or document.

ajouré
> A type of binding in which the leather is decorated with translucent, pierced, or open-work figures.

Albion Press
> An early wooden press invented by R. W. Cope of London in 1823. It is also called the Toggle Press because of its toggle-jointed lever mechanism--its main characteristic.

Aldine Bindings
> The term was originally applied to the early bindings of the Aldine Press, noted for the use of interlacing strapwork and tooling with solid-faced ornaments of Arabic design.

Aldus Classification System
> An early classification system, formulated by Aldus in 1498. In the catalog of Greek books, the five groups are divided according to their origin.

alfa
> Also called esparto; a grass produced in Spain and North Africa, used as a fiber for papermaking.

all-along sewing
> A very special kind of sewing which is done by hand. The thread is carried through the fold of the first section, around the tapes and cords from head to tail, across the next section by means of a kettle stitch, and up and down the entire back of the book.

almanac
In medieval times, an almanac was a permanent table showing
the movements of the heavenly bodies, from which calculations
for any year could be made. A further step, in the evolution of
the form, came with the inclusion of useful information, especially for farmers. This use of the almanac as a storehouse of
general fact led eventually to modern works, such as the World
Almanac, a compendium of historical and statistical data not
limited to the single year.

amanuensis
A person employed to write from dictation, or to copy what
another has written.

Americana
A collection of literary, ethnographic, historical, documentary
works, etc., relating to America; hence works relating to America or individual Americans, but not necessarily by Americans
or about America as such. The Bay Psalm Book, the first known
book printed in what is now America, is a piece of Americana.

American Copyright
First Federal Copyright Act   Passed in 1790, it covered the
publication of books, maps, and charts, and protected the
rights of Americans only. The period covered was fourteen
years, with a renewal period of fourteen years. The require-
ments were three: a copy of the title page of the work in question had to be deposited before publication; the seeker of copyright had to advertise the facts of publication in a newspaper
for four weeks during the two months immediately following
the publication; a copy of the work published had to be deposited at the office of the United States Secretary of State
within six months of publication.

The Chace Act of 1891   Extended copyright protection to
foreigners, the conditions being: the work bore an American
copyright; the title was registered at the Copyright Office;
two copies of the work were mailed on the day of publication.

Current status of American Copyright   Period of copyright is
now twenty-eight years, with a renewal period of twenty-eight
years. English books sold in the United States must be manufactured and bound in the United States to quality for copyright,

but foreign books printed in a foreign language need no longer be reprinted in America to qualify for an American copyright.

American Library Association
A national association, founded in 1876, which includes all the library associations of the United States. It has won general esteem for its efforts to unify and advance bibliographic, as well as library, work through its annual meetings, its committees, and its publications.

amulet
General sense: an ornament, gem, or scroll, or a packet containing a relic, etc., worn as a charm or preservative against evils or mischief, such as diseases and witchcraft, and often inscribed with a spell or magic incantation or symbol. Limited meaning: stone bearing short inscription and, often, name of the engraver.

ana
A collection, originally of the memorable sayings or table talk of a person; later of items of information relative to a subject of curious interest, such as Boswell's Johnson, the ana of all anas. The term also refers to items in or suitable for such a collection.

analytical bibliography
Seeks the answers to the following questions: (1) What work or works does the volume contain? (2) What edition of the work is this? (3) Is this a perfect copy?

anastatic
A process used chiefly in France in the nineteenth century for the producing of reprints. An inked offset of the type was made on a metal plate by means of an acid or corrosive, and then the metal plate was used to print copies.

annals
A relation of events in chronological order, each event being recorded under the year in which it happened. This practice developed into such records as the Anglo-Saxon chronicles. In modern times, the term annals is used loosely to designate periodic publications containing records of discoveries, transactions of societies, etc., such as Annals of Science, Annals of Congress, Annals of Music, Annals of Mathematics.

annual reviews
Bibliographic lists or catalogs which appear in completed books
periodically. They are especially common among trade catalogs.

annuals
Works appearing in successive numbers at intervals of one
year and usually reviewing the events of the year within the
specified fields of interest: as college annuals, Christmas
annuals. The term is sometimes applied also to compendiums,
such as the World Almanac.

anopisthographic
Block-books in which the woodcut text and figures are printed
on only one side of the leaf; loosely, having writing or printing
on one side only.

anthology
A collection of the flowers of literature, or beautiful passages
from authors. The term originally signified a collection of
about 4,500 short Greek poems dating between the Alexandrian
era and early medieval times. It now means simply selections
or extracts, in prose or verse, from the writings in any language of one or more than one author.

antiqua
Roman and similar types, derived from a tradition older than
the Gothic; another name for Caroline minescules or round
letters.

antiquary
Students of ancient times through their relics such as monuments, remains of ancient habitations, statues, coins, manuscripts, etc.; one who collects or studies antiquities.

antique
A paper of inferior quality, made from mixed esparto and
wood fibers; in printing, a style of display type; in bookbinding,
embossed or impressed without ink, foil, or gold--blank, blind.

applied bibliography
Also called "material bibliography," that is, external, des-
criptive, and historical. It treats books from the point of view
of purchase and sale, and in accordance with the special in-
clination of the compiler.

aquatint
> A process of etching in which spaces are bitten in with aqua fortis, producing an effect resembling a drawing in water colors or india ink; also, the engraving so produced. It was invented by Jean Baptist Le Prince (1734-1781).

archives
> A place in which public records or historic documents are kept; also, the public records or documents preserved as evidence of facts; as, national or family archives.

armarium
> A repository. In churches, a recess (formerly always a closed cupboard) made in a wall, to hold sacramental vessels, vestments, books, etc. The word derives from Armarius, a medieval librarian. A synonymous term, perhaps better known, is ambry.

armorial
> A book of heraldic arms; belonging to or bearing heraldic arms. A binding stamped with the coat of arms of its original or a subsequent owner; bookplates based on or incorporating the owner's arms.

art paper
> A paper coated, through brushing, with china clay, sulphate of barium, which sharply reproduces the excessively shallow relief of the halftone process.

ascender
> In printing, a letter which has a stroke rising above the body of the letter, such as the letter d or l, as against the letters a or e.

Ashley Catalogue
> An elaborate and lavishly illustrated catalogue of a great collection (subsequently purchased by the British Museum). Of special value to students of the Romantic and Pre-Raphaelite movements, since it contains matter relative to a large body of manuscript material and ana.

association copy
> A copy which once belonged to, or was annotated by, the

author; or once belonged to someone connected with the author or in some special way associated with the contents of the work.

author catalogue
A catalogue in which books, etc., are listed only under the names of the authors, editors, compilers, etc., usually arranged alphabetically.

author entry
In cataloguing, entry of a writing under the name (usually with surname first) of its author; also, an entry so made.

authorized edition
An appreciable number of 16th, 17th, and 18th century works were first printed without their author's consent or knowledge, sometimes from correct manuscripts, at other times from garbled or stolen ones. Serialized publications in the 19th century were particularly liable to piracy.

author's binding
From the earliest times, a work was occasionally bound in a special way, at the request of the author, for presentation to friends. A common style of binding for this purpose, in the 17th and 18th centuries, was panelled morocco; in an earlier period, it was vellum.

author's copyright
Legal right or privilege given to the author of a book to publish and sell his book.

autograph
In the author's own handwriting, as an autograph letter, an autograph will; also, a manuscript, a person's signature or handwriting. Common abbreviations are: A.L., autograph letter, unsigned; A.L.s., autograph letter, signed; L.s., letter in the hand of another, signed; T.L.s., typed letter, signed by hand; M.S., manuscript; MSS., manuscripts.

autotype
A picture made by the carbon process; a facsimile.

autotypography
A process resembling nature printing, by which drawings

executed on gelatin, are impressed into a soft metal plate,
from which the printing is done as from a copperplate.

autotypy
　　Process of making autotypes.

avon fount
　　A type especially designed by Charles Ricetts (England) in 1896
　　for his private press, The Vale Press.

azured binding tools. See ajouré.

# B

backed
　　Having a back or fitted with a back, as a backed electrotype,
　　backed leaves. In binding, a work the spine of which is covered
　　with a different material from that of the sides, the implication
　　being that the spine has been recovered.

back mark
　　A small oblong block that is printed in the margin, where the
　　outer fold of the first and last leaves of the sheet will be, in such
　　a position that, when the sheets are folded and piled for binding,
　　the oblongs follow each other in a slanting position or sequence
　　down the back of the book, thus showing at a glance an omission
　　or a duplication.

backstrip
　　The usually narrow portion of a book cover connecting the front
　　and back boards or sides; loosely, the spine or back of the book.

ball
　　In printing, a leather-covered or composition cushion, fastened

to a handle (the ballstock), formerly used for inking the form.

Ballantyne Press
An early private press in England.

Bangor Antiphonary
The earliest Irish manuscript which can be dated (circa 690),
so named from having been written at Bangor. (Antiphonary,
a book of verses sung in response; that is, the book in which
the antiphons of the breviary, with their musical notes, are
contained.)

bar
The lever by which the printing press was operated.

Barker's Bible
An octavo Bible published in 1631, famous for its injunction:
"Thou shalt commit adultery." It was ordered burnt by the
Court of High Commission.

barrel
The drum in the center of the rounce on a hand press.

Basle Roman Type
A font of type used at Basle by Johann Froben.

bas-relief
Sculpture in low relief, in which the figures protrude only
slightly from the background.

bastarda type
A Gothic printing type with looped ascenders and pointed des-
cenders, used in France until about 1520; known in France as
Lettre Batarde.

bastard title
An abbreviated title preceding the full title page; a half title.

bastard type
Type having the face larger or smaller than the size proper
to the body, as a nonpareil face on a brevier body; type not
on the point system.

Bay Psalm Book
   A psalter published at Cambridge, Massachusetts in 1640.
   Published by the Stephen Day Press, it was the first book
   printed in English in America.

bearer
   A ledge on either side of the bed of a cylinder press, to equalize
   the motion of the cylinder over the form; a track on either side
   of a platen press, upon which the end of an inking roller moves;
   a strip of wood or metal placed at either end of a chase for a
   platen press, to equalize the contact of the rollers with the
   type form during printing; in electrotyping, a guard line.

bed
   In printing, the part of the press on which the form is laid; in
   bookbinding, a water solution of gum tragacanth used as a couch
   in the process of marbling book edges; the impression base used
   in stamping, graining, or embossing covers or materials.

Behistun Inscription
   A cuneiform inscription, in three languages (Old Persian,
   Elamite, Assyrian), on a limestone mountain near the ruined
   town of Behistun, Persia. It recounts the genealogy and con-
   quests of Darius I (6th century B.C.). Its decipherment by Sir
   Henry Rawlinson furnished the key to our knowledge of Assyrian
   and Babylonian records.

belles-lettres
   Literature of aesthetic value, especially poetry, essays, drama,
   orations, or fiction characterized by emotional effect or ele-
   vated style;--distinguished from information or utilitarian
   writings. Formerly termed litterae humaniores.

belletrist, belle-lettrist
   A person devoted to belles-lettres.

bevelled edges
   A style of binding in which the edges of the boards, in this instance exceptionally thick boards, are cut to a slanting level
   before being covered.

Biblia del O'so
   The first published (1569) Spanish translation of the whole Bible,

so called from the bear which appeared as the frontispiece. It was published at Basel.

## Biblia Latina
A transitional Gothic-roman type of printing.

## Biblia Pauperum
One of a class of medieval books, representing in pictures the chief Old and New Testament events in man's salvation. It was one of the first books printed by block-book printing.

## Biblical Apocrypha
A collection of fourteen books in harmony with the Bible, which are accepted by the Roman Catholic Church and rejected by the Protestant Church. Some of these books are: (1) 1 and 2 Tesdra, (2) Tobit, (3) Judith, (4) Esther.

## Biblical criticism
The use of scholarly methods, either textual (lower criticism) or literary and historical (higher criticism), to determine the origin, nature, and meaning of the literature of the Bible.

## Biblical hand
A book hand of the Byzantine period (about 300-650 A.D.), characterized by squarish uncials of somewhat heavy appearance. The three chief codices of the Bible are written in it.

## Biblicism
Adherence to the letter of the Bible.

## Biblicist
One versed in the Bible; one who adheres to the letter of the Bible; specifically, one of the medieval doctors (sometimes called Biblical doctors) who demonstrated religious truths chiefly by means of the Bible.

## biblioclasm
Destruction of books, especially the Bible.

## biblioclast
A destroyer or mutilator of books.

## bibliogony
Production of books.

bibliographer
   A scribe or copyist; one who writes, or is versed in, bibliography.

bibliographic manual
   A handbook which lists the chief works in the field; combines
   a select bibliography and bibliographies of bibliographies.

bibliographic periodical
   A literary-critical periodical, frequently with bibliophilic
   tendencies, which contains some lists (titles), in addition to
   some theoretical matter on bibliography.

Bibliographical Society
   Founded in London by Copinger in 1892, its aims are to in-
   vestigate bibliography, publish bibliographical papers, and
   to build up a library of bibliography.

bibliography
   The art of recording books; the science which deals with the
   making of books and their extant record. The term was first
   used by Lewis Jacob de Saint Charles in 1645 and originally
   signified the mechanical writing and transcription of books,
   but not their composition. The term was later expanded to
   include composition. The three main divisions are: analytical,
   the bibliographical method in which laboratory work precedes
   classification; systematic, the bibliographical method in which
   book entries are assembled into logical and useful arrangements for reference and study; historical, the method--also
   called the "natural history method"--in which books are grouped
   according to their generic origin as well as chronologically.

bibliography--its value
   Helps to solve questions about the order and worth of different
   editions of a book: whether certain sections of a book were
   originally intended to form part of it or were added afterwards;
   whether a later edition was printed from an earlier one, and from
   which; whether it was printed from a copy that had been corrected
   in manuscript, or from a copy that had been corrected after the
   manuscript stage.

bibliography, universal
   The nearest approach to a universal bibliography is the catalogue

of a very large library. Ranked highest are the author and subject catalogues of the British Museum. This library also contains the greatest list of periodicals in existence.

bibliolatry
Worship of a book or books; worship of the Bible; submission
to a group of sacred writings as the plenary depository of the
Divine Spirit and, as such, infallible and authoritative.

bibliomania
Enthusiasm for collecting books, characterized by slight, if any,
concern for content. The bibliomaniac's primary, if not total,
preoccupation is with the form, association, or accidental
rarity of books.

bibliopegic
Relating to the binding of books.

bibliopegy
The art of binding books.

bibliophile
Fancier or lover of books, especially of their format.

bibliophilism
Love of books.

bibliopolism
The trade or art of selling books.

Biblioteca Ambrosiana
Cardinal Federigo Borromeo (1564-1631) started his collection
of books as a boy, and opened his library to the public in its
own building in 1609. At his death, the library contained over
30,000 volumes, many of them extremely rare, including some
15,000 manuscripts. It remains today one of Italy's finest
libraries.

Biblioteca Laurentiana
Originally the library of Giulio dei Medici, subsequently Pope
Clement VII. In 1521, he gave his library to Florence and commissioned Michelangelo to construct a building to house it. It
was completed as the Laurentian Library in 1571.

Biblioteca Marciana
> The National Library in Venice, originally begun with the col-
> lection donated by Cardinal Bessarion in 1468. It contains only
> about a half million printed volumes, but has some of the rarest
> medieval codices and over 13,000 invaluable manuscripts.

Biblioteca Saviliana
> A collection given to the Bodleian Library by one of Sir Thomas
> Bodley's close friends. It contains a large number of Greek and
> Latin manuscripts, on topics including geometry and astronomy.

bibliothec
> A library or librarian. Also bibliothecary.

bibliotheca
> A library; also bibliotheke.

bibliothecal bibliography
> A phase of bibliography concerned with the collection, preser-
> vation, and organization of books in libraries (library science
> and the history of libraries). It supplies the answer to the
> questions: where are these books, and how can we get to them?

Bibliotheque Mazarine
> One of the greatest private libraries in France in the seventeenth
> century was that of Cardinal Mazarin. In 1660, his collection
> numbering over 45,000 volumes, he founded the library of the
> College Mazarin, destined, in time, to become one of the most
> famous libraries in Paris.

Bibliotheque Nationale
> The French national library. By 1860 it possessed a million and
> a half volumes and was already one of the foremost libraries in
> the world. By 1960 it had well over 5,000,000 volumes, not in-
> cluding its many thousands of manuscripts, cartographs, en-
> gravings, and pictures. It remains one of the world's great
> libraries.

Bibliotheque Ste. Genevieve
> One of the five major libraries of the University of Paris, the
> other four being the Sorbonne, which now serves as the library
> of the college of arts and sciences; and the libraries of the
> Faculty of Medicine, the Faculty of Law, and the Faculty of

of Pharmacy. The Ste. Genevieve Library is probably the oldest
of the five libraries, dating from the twelfth century. By 1860 it
claimed 160,000 printed books and 5,000 manuscripts; by 1900
the library possessed some 350,000 volumes, including one of
the most valuable collections on the history of France and
Europe.

Biblism
Adherence to the Bible as the sole rule of faith.

Biblist
A teacher or student of the Bible; one who makes the Bible the
sole rule of faith; a biblical scholar; a biblicist.

biblus
Papyrus.

binder's board
A smooth, hard, tough pulpboard much used in covers by bookbinders.

binder's cloth
Cotton fabric with a finish suitable for book covers.

binder's title
The title printed or stamped by the binder on the outside of the
cover of a book.

binder twine
A coarse slack-twisted twine or thin rope used in binding,
especially in tying grain after cutting.

binding
the process of folding, trimming and assembling various elements of a printed folder, brochure, or book.

decorated binding    The decorating of books in different styles,
such as La Gascon Binding, Scottish Binding, Eighteenth-Century
French Dentelle Binding.

finishing binding    The second half of the binding process, which
includes the final touches, such as lettering, decorating, etc.

forwarding  The first half of the binding process, which in-cludes everything necessary to make a secure unit of book and cover.

half-binding  The back and the outer corners of the boards are covered with leather; the rest of the boards are covered with paper or cloth.

library binding  The same as luxurious binding; includes care-ful sewing to insure that the book does not fall apart. While it involves the use of definite standards, it does not demand the fine skin surfaces that are required for luxurious binding.

quarter binding  Only the spine is leather covered.

sewing  Consists of threads running perpendicularly up and passing through the fold in the middle of each section to hold the pairs of leaves in each section together; and cords or tapes, around or through the threads, are passed to hold the section together, running across the back of the book.

three-quarter binding  The leather covers the spine and one-third of each cover.

whole-binding  All the outside of the book, covers and back, is covered with leather.

binding variants
Relative to differences of color, fabric, lettering, or decoration between different copies of the same edition, the result of books being bound as needed; that is, at different times, rather than in a single operation.

Bingham Library
There were few public libraries in the United States before 1850. In Salisbury, Connecticut, however, a collection of books donated in 1803 by Caleb Bingham was preserved and made available by the town as the Bingham Library for youth. It sur-vived to become a part of the modern Scoville Memorial Library.

bite
A term given when the edge of a frisket sheet was caught between the type and the paper; when this happened, the frisket was said to bite.

black-letter
> A style of letter or of type characterized by black face and angular outlines, which was imitated by the early printers from a current manuscript letter. It still prevails in Germany, and in English-speaking countries is in occasional use in the form known as Old English or (in British usage) Gothic.

blank leaves
> They are part of the full sheet. Although unprinted on, they must be left in the book for its perfection.

bleed
> To trim the edge of a page so as to cut into printed or engraved matter; said of page margins, printed covers, plates, etc. In the case of engraved matter, the tone is sometimes purposely extended beyond the edge to be trimmed.

blind tooling
> The prevailing form of binding decoration until the end of the 15th century, to tool without gilding or coloring. It is done by pressing deeply cut metal stamps on to the binding leather, which has been dampened and softened.

Bliss Collection
> Collected by Dr. Philip Bliss, it includes: books printed at Oxford; books of characters; books printed in London during the three years preceding the Great Fire; versions and commentaries on the Psalms; works of "Royal and Noble Authors"; and works of sixteenth- and seventeenth-century poets.

block
> A piece of boxwood or other wood for engravers' work; an engraved block or stamp from which impressions are made, as on cloth or paper; a piece of hard wood or metal on which a stereotype, electrotype, or engraved plate is mounted to make it type-high; a bookbinder's stamp too large for handwork; the wooden core of a lithographer's roller.

block, to
> To emboss book covers with a frame or block containing the entire device; also (in the United States), to stamp.

block-book
> In the early stages of printing, one process was accomplished from an inked surface formed by cutting on a wooden block the lines of the original design in reverse, and then cutting away the background so that the raised design was left as the printing surface. Nearly all of the "block-books" were of a popular and pious nature, consisting mainly of crude pictures with a text limited to labels and simple explanations of what was illustrated. As the pictures were printed on only one side, the sheets were pasted back-to-back, so that only the printed matter was visible on opening the books. A typical block-book is the Biblia Pauperum.

Bodleian Library
> The library of Oxford University, established by Thomas de Cobham in 1410. About 1660 it was restored by Sir Thomas Bodley and reopened in 1602. A great non-lending library, the Bodleian is particularly strong in early books and manuscripts, and is an excellent research center for the scholar.

body size
> The size of a type on its vertical axis (also called type size).

bolt
> A printed and folded but untrimmed signature.

book-building
> The process of book production, including the steps of composition, correction, printing, folding, and binding.

book clamp
> A clamp to hold or press books, as for binding or marbling.

book cloth
> Any of several specially woven fabrics, usually cotton, prepared for use in covering books.

book fell
> A sheet or manuscript of vellum or parchment.

book hand
> Remarkably uniform handwriting used by professional scribes during the Old English and Middle English periods. Because

these men wrote with much care, older manuscripts are easier to read than those dating from the period 1500-1600.

book jacket
A detachable paper cover, usually attractively illustrated, protecting the binding of the book.

bookman
A style of type.

Book of Canons
A code of canons for the Church of Scotland (1636). It asserted the royal supremacy and required a new service book and a complete episcopal organization.

Book of Common Order, The
The service book used in the Church of Scotland from the Reformation until 1645, originally drawn up by John Knox.

Book of Common Prayer
The service book of the Anglican Communion, being mainly a compilation and translation of pre-Reformation liturgical material, made chiefly by Cranmer, and first published in 1549, being the First Prayer Book of Edward VI.

Book of Concord
A collection of confessions of faith, generally accepted by Lutheran churches. It was published in 1580.

Book of Discipline
Any one of several important directories of Presbyterian Church government.

Book of Homilies
Either of two collections of sermons, designed to popularize Protestantism in the Church of England, the first edited by Cranmer in 1547, the second by Jewel in 1563.

Book of Hours
A book containing prayers or offices appointed to be said at the canonical hours; famous for its three-hundred paintings of plants and insects, its forty-nine miniatures from the Old Testament

and the New Testament, and for its calendar. Written by Anne
of Brittany (circa 1498).

Book of Kells
An elaborately illuminated manuscript of the Gospels in Latin,
with certain local records, in the Irish Celtic style of the 7th
to the 9th centuries, preserved in the library of Trinity College,
Dublin. Probably the most beautiful manuscript in existence.

Book of Martyrs
An account of religious persecutions, especially in England,
from 64 A.D. to 1558, inclusive, when Queen Mary died. It
was written by John Foxe and first printed in Latin in 1559; in
English, in 1563.

Book of the Dead
An old manuscript written on papyrus, exhumed from ancient
Egyptian graves. A collection of formulas, prayers, and hymns,
knowledge of which was believed to enable the soul to successfully pass by its foes on its journey to the region of the dead.

bookplate
A label placed upon or in a book, showing its ownership or its
position in a library; an ex libris; also, an engraved plate for
printing such a label.

book sizes
To determine the number of pages cut from the original foolscap
of 17" by 13 1/2" one counts the number of pages to a "signature"; this is often done by noting the number of occurrences
of the signature marks which appear at regular intervals at the
foot of the page. These symbols are usually numerals or letters and may be found regularly in early printed books and
sometimes in recently printed ones. They indicate the beginning
of new signatures. The number of leaves (not pages) in a single
signature shows the number of leaves cut from the original
sheet and is, therefore, the indication of the book size. Some
typical book sizes are: two leaves and four pages, folio; four
leaves and eight pages, quarto; eight leaves and sixteen pages,
octavo; twelve leaves and twenty-four pages, duodecimo;
sixteen leaves and thirty-two pages, sixteenmo; thirty-two
leaves and sixty-four pages, thirty-twomo; sixty-four leaves
and one hundred and twenty-eight pages, sixty-fourmo.

border
> A plain or decorative band or panel along the edge or around
> the edges of a body of type matter; also, a unit of type material
> for producing such bands or panels.

Boston Athenaeum Library
> In the nineteenth century it was in a class by itself as a histor-
> ical society library. When it moved into a new building in 1849,
> by which time it already possessed over 50,000 volumes, it
> ranked with Harvard and the Library of Congress as the largest
> libraries in the United States.

Boston News Letter
> First American newspaper.

Boston Public Library
> By 1877 it contained nearly 300,000 volumes and circulated
> over a million volumes a year and was the most important
> public library in America.

bowdlerize
> To expurgate a book or piece of writing by omitting all offensive
> or indecorous passages. The term derives from the name of
> Thomas Bowdler, an English physician, who published an ex-
> purgated edition of Shakespeare in 1818.

Bradshaw Method
> Henry Bradshaw first applied the "natural history method" to
> the study of books. Developed in 1866, his method followed
> the same direction of thought as that of Darwin.

break
> In typefounding, a rough jet of metal on the shank as cast,
> which is removed in finishing.

breakers
> Devices used in the processing of chemical wood pulp, which
> separate the individual pulp fibers from each other.

breviary
> A book containing the daily public or canonical prayers for the
> canonical hours. The breviary of the Catholic Church has
> separate parts for the four seasons, each containing the order,

the psalter, the proper of the season, the proper of the saints, the common of the saints, et cetera.

Breviary of Alaric
An important collection of Roman laws, compiled by order of Alaric II, king of the Visigoths, and promulaged in 596 A.D.

brevier
A size of type (eight points).

British Museum Leather Dressing
A chemical preparation used to preserve leather bindings, con-sidered to be the best preservative devised.

British Museum Library
Regarded by some as the most important library in the world, strong in every department--manuscripts, books, and prints, on every subject of importance and in almost every language. It was founded in 1753. In 1754 the British Museum Library acquired the Harleian and the Cottonian collections which, along with the 1757 donation by George II of the royal library of the kings of England, constituted the core of the library.

broadsheet
A broadside.

broadside
A sheet of paper containing one large page, or printed on one side only; also called broadsheet.

Brook Type
A type, especially designed by Lucien Pissaro (England) for use in his Eragny Press--a private press.

Brown's Library
One of America's best known book collections. The library, particularly strong in early Americana, travels, and explor-ations, was kept intact and passed on to Brown University in 1900. (See John Carter Brown.)

Brussels Auxiliary Tables
These are supplements to the main Brussels system, used to indicate special features of a publication rather than its con-

tent. They are based on a fixed set of numerals, not capable
of extension, separated from the rest of the notation, in order
to indicate the form, the purpose, or the language of a published
work, regardless of whether or not these appear on the title
page.

Brussels Classification Scheme
An expansion and revision of the Dewey system. Apart from
a number of changes in the bases, the chief external difference
between the two schemes lies in the fact that the Dewey notations,
in spite of their occasional length, are always relatively simpler
in type than are the Brussels notations; that is, they always
represent an unbroken series of consecutive numbers, whereas
the Brussels system occurs in groups, several groups separated
from each other in various ways.

Brussels Institute  The Institut International de Bibliographie
Organized in Brussels in 1895, it is an international association
of learned societies and scholars, designed primarily to serve
the objectives of documentation. It has branched into all the
areas of bibliography.

buckram
A coarse, cotton hemp or linen cloth stiffened with glue or a
glue-like substance, used in the binding process.

bulk
In the manufacture of paper, it signifies the thickness of a
specified number of sheets of paper; in bookbinding, it signifies
the thickness of the book without the cover.

Bulletin of Bibliography
Keeps a current record of the "births and deaths" in the world
of periodicals.

bumper
In machine binding, a mechanical apparatus which applies pressure to assembled books, to consolidate or compact them.

Byzantine Bindings
A highly artistic book decoration, introduced in the fourth
century, initially characterized by smoothness and the use of

unadorned oak boards; later, by book covers wrought in gold and silver and often inlaid with precious stones.

# C

calligraphy
> The art or profession of producing fair or elegant writing, as that of the scribes of the Middle Ages.

Cambridge University Library
> One of the great university libraries of the world, second only, perhaps, to the Bodleian Library.

cameo stamps
> A tool with decorative pattern, used in blind tooling. The patterns on the stamp varied from country to country.

camisia
> A shirt or tunic, as an alb or rochet; a case or covering for a sacred object; a cover for a box in which a codex or scroll was kept.

cancel
> A leaf in which some correction or expurgation or other revision has been made, so that the binder may cut out the original leaf and substitute the cancel. The leaf replaced by a cancel is called a cancellandum.

Canevari Bindings
> A kind of binding, popular in Italy during the first-half of the 16th century. It consisted of a blind-tooled center panel, enclosing a sunken portion bearing a large cameo. It took its name from Demetrio Canevari, who inherited a large collection of books decorated in this manner.

**cap**
> In bookbinding, a paper covering placed over the gold edges of
> fine books until they are bound; in printing, the cross-piece at
> the top of the frame of the printing press, which held the cheeks
> about one foot and nine inches apart.

**capitals**
> The large decorative letters at the beginning of chapters.

**Caracters de civilite**
> A script type of 1557, which sought to imitate a Gothic cursive
> handwriting in vogue at the time.

**Carolingian or Caroline minuscule**
> A minuscule book hand developed in France in the eighth
> century (according to some, by Emperor Charlemagne)
> from the roman cursive, much influenced by the English half
> uncial. Its simple fluent letters supplanted all other western
> European alphabets, except in Ireland, where the Irish uncial
> persists. The Carolingian minuscule is the prototype of the
> modern styles of penmanship and of the printing typeface
> known as lower-case roman.

**carrell**
> In order to facilitate reading and writing in the cloister through-
> out the year, many of the English monasteries, which seldom
> had special rooms for libraries and scriptoria before the end
> of the 14th and the beginning of the 15th centuries, screened
> off one of the four cloister walks, filled in the window spaces
> with oiled paper, rush mats, or glass, and built several parti-
> tions, usually of wood, in front of each window to protect the
> scribes from the elements. These small partitioned studies,
> containing a desk and a seat beneath a cloister window, were
> called carrells. Today, a small enclosure or alcove in the
> stack room of a library, designed as a place for individual
> study or reading.

**carriage**
> The part of the printing press on which was fastened the forme
> of type which was to be printed.

cartobiography
A history or description of printed maps.

cartography
Art or business of drawing or making charts or maps.

cartonnage
Pasteboard, such as that used in binding books; also, the material of which many Egyptian mummy cases are made, consisting of linen glued together in many thickness and usually having a coating of stucco.

case
In bookbinding, a book cover that is made complete before it is affixed to a book; in electrotyping, a flat metal plate having on one side a layer of wax which, when impressed, forms a mold for an electrotype; in printing, a shallow tray or cabinet divided into compartments called "boxes," for holding type. Cases for body type are usually arranged in sets of two, called respectively the upper case and the lower case. The upper case contains capitals, small capitals, accented and marked letters, fractions, and marks of reference, consisting in all of ninety-eight boxes of uniform size in alphabetical arrangement. The lower case contains the small letters, figures, marks of punctuation, quadrats, and spaces. A pair of cases, always used together, constitute a font.

case binding
A process of bookbinding in which the book is fastened into a case; that is, the assembly of spine and case.

case bound
Having a case binding.

Caslon
A style of type originally designed by the English typefounder, William Caslon (1692-1766).

caster
The second step (or machine) which casts the letters from the punched paper.

casting
    Forming a mould in order that moulten metal can be poured,
    producing the printing surface.

catalogue
    A list or enumeration of names, titles, or articles arranged
    methodically, often in alphabetical order and usually with
    descriptive details, number, or price accompanying each item;
    also, a book or pamphlet containing such a list, together with
    other information, as a university, library, or museum catalogue.

catchword entry
    A title entry (as of a book) in a catalogue, list, or index, begin-
    ning with a significant or easily remembered word in the title
    (Inquisition, A history of the); also, the method of such entry.

catchwords
    The first word, or part of a word, found at the foot of the
    preceding page to aid the printer in imposing the pages cor-
    rectly. They were also additional signatures giving the volume
    numbers, used usually on the first leaf of a gathering in 18th-
    and 19th-century books printed in several volumes. These
    prevented sheets from getting mixed by the binder with those
    belonging to the other volumes. The catchword is seldom used
    in modern printing. The term also signifies the word standing
    at the head of an entry in a dictionary, concordance, etc., or
    either of the words printed over the first and last columns of
    a page of a dictionary, encyclopedia, etc., being reprints of
    the headings of the first and last entries or articles on the page.

Cathedral Bindings
    Those, popular in France and England between 1815 and 1840,
    which were decorated with Gothic architectural motifs.

cellulose pulp
    The end result of the processing of rags for papermaking
    purposes.

center headings
    Sometimes called captions, these are located in the body of the
    chapters to mark the different subdivisions therein. Paragraphs,
    for example, may begin with a heading in boldface type, italics,

or in small capitals. The lowest grade center heading is the
side heading, printed in the margin, often in italics. Center
headings help to reveal the logical arrangements or subordi-
nations.

Chace Act
A copyright act passed in America in 1891. It extended copyright protection to foreigners.

chained books
It is commonly believed that all books were chained in medieval
libraries. In many libraries, however, only certain books, such
as those used for reference, were chained. Moreover, it is
doubtful if the practice extended beyond the fifteenth century.

chain-lines
Five or six lines which run horizontally across the page where
the paper appears to be thinner than elsewhere, due to the
wire mold in which the paper was made.

chancery hand
A late variety of English court hand; a style of cursive used
by papal secretaries, from the middle of the 15th century,
and imitated in early italic type.

chancery type
Italic or script type developed in the fifteenth century by the
printer Aldus of Venice.

chapbook
Any small book or pamphlet containing ballads, tracts, etc.,
such as were sold to the common people in the sixteenth and
following centuries by peddlers or "chapmen." They are of
interest to the literary historian because of their reflection
of contemporary attitudes towards themes and situations treated
in literature.

chapter drop
The distance between the top of the page and the first part of
the chapter head.

Charta Pergamena
A special kind of parchment prepared from the skin of sheep,

goats, and pigs. It was first made by King Eumenes of Pergamun, when he found that he was unable to get papyrus from Egypt.

chartulary
> A collection or register of charters; especially, the book or case in which are contained duplicates of all charters, title deeds, etc., as of monastery or other landowner. A keeper of archives.

chase
> A bottomless frame large enough to contain all of the galleys to be printed at one time. In earlier times, it may have been a shallow box in which the compositor set up the type directly without using the composing stick. Today, it usually signifies a rectangular steel or iron frame into which pages or columns are fastened for printing or to make plates.

Chaucer Type
> A type designed by William Morris (nineteenth-century English poet and artist) for use in his private printing press, the Kelmscott Press.

checklist
> A list, usually alphabetic and numbered, of species, genera, etc., for the convenience of collectors and students, usually limited to a given group, region, or collection.

Checklist
> An index, issued by the Superintendent of Documents, which provides a complete inventory list of the documents, under: (a) American State Papers, (b) The Congressional Documents of the 15th to the 60th Congress (1817-1909), (c) Department publications. If one has knowledge of the approximate date of some departmental publication, he can almost always find a description of it in the Checklist.

cheeks
> The two side posts, 8" x 4 1/2" in depth and thickness, of the upright frame of the hand printing press, which stood about six feet high.

chemical wood
> A good quality of paper produced from fibers from wood

chips boiled under pressure in a solution of caustic soda.

chiaroscuro

A very early form of wood engraving and printing in which separate blocks were used to give the tints or hues; this is to say, the color masses were obtained by the successive printing, in register, of a number of subsidiary blocks.

china paper

A very thick and silky paper, used for woodcut proofs.

Chiswick Press

A remarkable English publishing-printing alliance, formed by William Pickering (publisher) and Charles Whittingham (printer), in 1828.

chrestomathy

A selection of passages, especially with notes, etc., to be used in learning a language.

chromolithograph

A colored picture printed from a series of stone or zinc plates, the impression from each plate being in a different color.

chromotype

A sheet printed in colors by any process.

chromotypography

The art of printing in chromatic colors.

chromoxylography

Printing in colors from wooden blocks.

chronicle

A form of historical writing. According to one authority, a chronicle differs from an annual in its comprehensive or universal character, its concern with world history; also, a bare and simple chronological record of events.

chronogram

A motto which contains the edition date of the book embedded, in roman numerals, within the words. The date is distinguished by being printed in either upper case or wrong font; more generally, an inscription, sentence, or phrase in which certain numeral letters, usually made specially conspicuous, on being added together express a particular date or epoch.

chronology
As used by students of literary research, the science of determining the dates of events of literary significance; generally used, an arrangement, as of date, events, or the like, in the order of the time of occurrence--chronological relation.

Cicero Type
A form designed by Claude Garamonde, one of the most distinguished French type designers in the sixteenth century. Of the three Greek type forms which he designed, the smallest size is known as the Cicero Type.

Civilité Type
A form designed by Robert Granjon in 1557. It was first introduced at Lyons and was based upon a cursive Gothic handwriting which was in vogue at the time.

clay tablets
Were used by the Babylonians and Assyrians in place of papyrus and skins. The cuneiform clay tablet, the earliest form of book, had an outer shell of clay on which was inscribed the copy, abstract, or title of the content.

clog almanacs
Squared pieces of wood, two feet or less in length and often three inches square, which have notches representing the days of the week. They were used in Elizabethan England.

clump
A slug of lead, six and twelve points thick or greater.

coated paper
A paper faced with a surface coating (as of china clay and an adhesive) and made smooth by calendering, that is, by being pressed in a roller machine.

codex
A wooden tablet covered with wax which, used for writing, constitutes the form of the earliest books; hence a manuscript

book, or an ancient manuscript, as of the Scriptures or the classics. Codices written in the Greek minuscule book hand, from the ninth century to the invention of printing, are clas- sified as: (1) codices vetustissimi (literally the oldest codices), those written from the ninth to the middle of the tenth century; (2) codices vetusti (old codices), those written from the middle of the thirteenth century; (3) codices recentiores (more recent codices), those written from the middle of the thirteenth century to the fall of Constantinople in 1453; (4) codices novelli (new codices), those written after the fall of Constantinople.

Codex Aaron Ben Asher
The Former and Latter Prophets in ninth-century Hellenic, preserved in Cairo.

Codex Alexandrinus
A fifth-century Greek manuscript, preserved in London and containing nearly the entire New Testament, in which the words and sentences are all joined together. When it was presented to Charles I in 1627, it was believed to be the oldest surviving text of the Greek Bible.

Codex Amiatinus
An eight-century Latin Bible preserved in Florence, Italy.

Codex Argenteus
The Gospels in eight-century Gothic, preserved in Uppsala.

Codex Bezae
Contains the four Gospels and Acts of the Apostles in Greek and Latin on opposite pages. They were written in the fifth or sixth century and are preserved in Cambridge.

Codex Boernerianus
Contains the Pauline Epistles in Greek and Latin. They were written in the ninth century and are preserved in Dresden.

Codex Claromontanus
The Pauline Epistles (in part) in Greek and Latin; written in the sixth century and preserved in Paris.

Codex Ephraemi Rescriptus
Contains portions of the Old Testament and New Testament

in Greek. Written in the fifth century; preserved in Paris.

Codex Gregorianus
Made privately about 300 A.D. by one Gregorianus (or, according to Mommsen, by Gregorius), of which only fragments are known.

Codex Hermogenian
Privately compiled, apparently as a supplement to the Gregorian code, and enacted probably about 365 A.D.

Codex Laudianus
Acts of the Apostles (in part) in Greek and Latin. Written in the sixth century; preserved in Oxford.

Codex Regius
The Gospels (in part). Written in Greek in the eighth century; preserved in Paris.

Codex Sangallensis
The Gospels in Greek and Latin. Written in the ninth or tenth century; preserved in St. Gallen.

Codex Sinaiticus
Undoubtedly the single most valuable acquisition ever made by the trustees of the British Museum Library. It is datable by its uncial script to the fourth century. It was found in 1844 by Tischendorf in the monastery of St. Catherine on Mount Sinai in a heap of unbound parchment leaves. It was first purchased by the Tsar of Russia from the monks of St. Catherine for 9,000 rubles. In 1933, the Soviet Government offered it to England for 100,000 pounds, a sum raised by public subscription.

Codex Vaticanus
The Bible (in part) in Greek. Written in the fourth century; it is preserved in Rome. The term Vaticanus is generally employed to signify one of the important manuscripts of the Vatican Library.

codicil
An instrument made subsequently to a will and modifying it in some respects. It must be executed in the same manner as

the will itself, and forms a part of it. In the Roman canon, and early English law, a kind of informal will made without the appointment of executors, normally held to be essential to a valid will. It was by codicil that many collections of printed books and manuscripts were bequeathed to libraries in earlier times.

coeval documents
One type of evidence concerning the origin of printing in Europe. The term applies to documents of the same or equal age or antiquity.

coffin
A rectangular frame, twenty-eight inches long, twenty-inches wide, and two and one-half inches deep, in which was embedded a smooth stone of limestone or marble, which was called the press-stone. Upon this the chase was laid.

collate
To examine a set of sheets or a book to verify the order and number of signatures, pages, plates, maps, etc.

collation
The technical description of a book including pagination, format, signatures, and plates; that is, the examination of the sheets of a book which is to be bound in order to insure that the pages, plates, indices, etc., are in the proper order; the act of comparing a book or set of sheets or signatures.

colophon
A separate paragraph at the end of the book giving the place of printing, the date, and information as to by or for whom the book was printed. By 1530, this information was transferred to the title page, and the colophon gradually went out of use.

collotype
A process whereby sensitized glass is exposed through a negative to produce a plate which can be inked. The photographic plate is made from gelatin film in such a manner that inked reproductions can be printed from it. With processes such as engraving, photogravure, and lithography, anything that can be photographed can be reproduced; nonetheless, the collotype process is more

purely photographic than these. The printing surface is a photo-graphic "positive," placed over either glass or metal; the grain of the process is fine enough for scientific reproductions re-quiring high detailing.

colporteur
A hawker; one who distributes or sells religious tracts and books. In early times, the peddler or itinerant bookseller who sold chap books, almanacs, religious works, and other books of a very popular nature.

common-law right
Rather vague predecessor of the copyright.

commonplace book
A book containing memoranda of passages or events for refer-ence. The term is also applied to private collections of favorite pieces of literature, such as the poetical miscellanies of Eliz-abethan times.

Company of Stationers
A printing establishment which existed since the beginning of the 15th century. In 1556, it was incorporated and given the monopoly of printing, by Royal Charter, in order to concentrate printing under the eye of authority. It was ordered to keep a register of the copies licensed by the Bishop of London; hence came into existence the foundation stone of English bibliography, the Stationers' Register, now available in print from its in-ception to 1708.

compartment
A distinction of one group of borders: (1) a carved or engraved single piece with the center portion cut out so that the piece resembles an empty picture; (2) an enclosure originally carved or engraved as above, but later cut into four or more pieces; (3) four or more pieces carved or engraved separately, but evidently intended to form part of a single design when as-sembled; (4) borders made from four pieces of cast type-ornaments, when the ends were cut obliquely, so that the only possible use for the piece was to help form a border.

Complutension Polyglot Bible
Printed in 1513-1517 at Complutum (now Alcala de Henares),

it contains the Old Testament in Hebrew, the Targum of Onkelos on the Pentatech, the Septuagint, the Vulgate, and the Greek New Testament. One of the four great Bible polyglots. Another is the Antwerp Polyglot, or Biblia Regia, which appeared in 1569-1572.

compose
  Printing, to arrange type in a composing stick in order to prepare for transference to galley; to set type.

composing rule
  A type-high strip of brass or steel, with ears at the upper corners, against which type is set and transferred to the galley.

composing stick
  A tray, usually of metal, which the compositor holds in his left
  hand, and in which he arranges the type in words and lines. It
  has a sliding piece which can be set to the required length of the
  line.

composition
  The process of setting types or characters in the composing
  stick to form lines; of arranging the lines in a galley to make
  a column or page; and from this, to make a form.

compositor
  The man who sets up the type for printing when the process is
  done by hand.

concept bibliography
  A list of material concerning only one specific subject.

concordance
  An alphabetical verbal index showing the places in the text of
  a book, or in the works of an author, where each principal
  word may be found, often with its immediate context in each
  place.

conjugate leaves
  two leaves which form a single sheet of paper.

consute
  The leaves of a book collectively that are folded and stitched
  into one quire. Another term for "gathering."

copper engraving
   An intaglio method of illustration introduced in 1477. The outline of the design is first sketched on a sheet of paper and is
   then worked upon a waxed copper plate. The plate is then engraved with a graver. The ridges are removed with a scraper
   to get a clear line. After the processes of inking, polishing,
   etc., the design is printed on paper.

Coptic
   The language and literature of ancient Egyptian in its latest
   stages, with numerous Greek loan words, and dating from the
   2d century A.D. It is divided into five main dialects. It became
   a dead language about 1500 A.D., but is still in use as the
   liturgical language of the Coptic Church.

Coptic sewing
   The earliest form of sewing books, which consisted of multiple
   sections, through which were passed a sewing thread up the
   fold of each gathering from the hole in the fold at the end. These
   ends were then tied together, to secure the sections to each
   other.

copyright
   The exclusive right to reproduce (by writing, printing, or otherwise), publish, and sell the matter and form of a literary or
   artistic work in various other ways (dramatizing, novelizing,
   motion pictures, etc.). The term of copyright is 28 years, with
   right of renewal for 28 years on due application, with a corresponding renewal right as to existing copyrights obtained under
   previous statutes.

copyright depository lists
   Lists of those books and other materials, copyrighted in a particular country during a designated period of time.

cornua
   Projecting knobs, also called umbilici. They were part of the
   wooden rollers that held the continuous sheets of ancient manuscripts which were preserved around a wooden roller.

Costeriana
   Some rudely printed books in a year earlier than 1440 by an inventor of printing named Laurens Coster.

cottage binding
    A form of Restoration binding in which there is a center panel
    with a gable at the top, or at both top and bottom.

coucher
    An instrumental part of the hand press, which stacked the new-
    ly made sheets of paper between sheets of felt.

crayon etching
    A method of etching using a roulette to copy the design, making
    each line to be a row of fine dots.

Crerar Library
    One of two major research libraries in Chicago, Illinois. It
    was begun in 1895 as a scientific library to balance and complete
    the work begun by the Newberry collection. In 1960, it had ap-
    proximately a million volumes. It is now housed in a new build-
    ing on the grounds of the Illinois Institute of Technology.

criblé
    A kind of engraving, used in the 15th century, in which round
    holes in the block or plate produce white spots in the print.

critical edition
    An edition intended for scholars which represents the author's
    final intentions, with all errors eliminated, difficult allusions
    explained, and a commentary which serves to fit the work into
    its setting.

crown privileges
    The earliest form of publisher's copyright, prevalent during
    the 1500's, which emanated from the British Crown and lasted
    for several years.

crown sheet
    A sheet of paper, called the "large folio," which measures
    fifteen inches by twenty inches.

cryptography
    The act or art of writing in cipher; that is, substituting one
    word or letter for another to conceal the real meaning.

cue words
> Those words from the title or content of a work, under which
> the work is classified in any of the various catalogs, lists, or
> indexes.

cuir bouilli
> Leather, softened by boiling or soaking, is pressed or molded
> into shape, and hardened by drying. It was used in the middle
> ages for armor; was a method of blind tooling practiced in
> Germany in the 15th century; and is now used especially for
> decorative objects.

cuir ciselé
> An ancient style of decorative bookbinding made on leather
> covers by outlining with a knife and stippling the uncut back-
> ground.

cumdachs
> The caskets or book-shrines where monastic manuscripts with
> simple bindings were kept.

Cumulative Book Index
> An American book trade periodical founded in 1898 by the H.
> W. Wilson Company.

cuneiform
> An early form of writing, thought to have originated with the
> Sumerians about 6000 years ago, consisting of wedge-shaped
> strokes made by pressing the end of a stick or reed into the
> soft clay of the tablet at an angle and continuing the stroke in a
> straight line with constantly diminishing pressure. From the
> Sumerians, cuneiform writing spread widely, remaining in
> use until the 3rd century B.C. The chief cuneiform signaries
> or syllabaries are the Sumerian, Assyro-Babylonian or Akkadian,
> Hittite, Hurrian, Vannic, Susian, and Old Persian. Of these,
> the oldest is the Sumerian, with ideographic characters; the
> most important, in extent and length of use, is the Assyro-
> Babylonian.

cuneus
> Literally, a wedge; the wedge-shaped space between panels and
> walls; a corner used for books; a nook.

cup and ring markings
> Rock inscriptions in the form of groups of rings and concentric circles which are connected. Such markings have been found from Ireland to India.

cursive
> A kind of printing type resembling handwriting. A good example of cursive type is the <u>Kunstrich Buch</u> printed by Christoph Fraschauer at Zurich, 1567.

Cutter number
> Named after Charles Cutter (1837-1903), librarian of Newberry Library. A combination of characters representing an author's surname, composed of the initial letter or the first letters, followed by numbers, chosen to make the numerical order of the symbols correspond with the alphabetical order of the names, and used to arrange books in the same class alphabetically by authors.

cylinder papermaking machine
> First used in 1809, its mechanism involved cylinders which helped to form the paper and to get it pressed and dried.

cylinder press
> A printing press in which the impression is produced by a revolving cylinder; also, one in which the form of type or plates is curved around a cylinder.

# D

dandy
> A special roller, used to watermark in machine-made paper, which revolves over the mould and impresses at every revolution upon the moving pulp the device which is in relief upon it.

dating editions
>To establish the chronological order of editions, one examines the chronogram, and considers the known date of the printer, the type used, etc.

Day Press
>Published the first book in America, the <u>Bay</u> <u>Psalm</u> <u>Book</u> (1640). Stephen Daye was the first printer in America.

Dead Sea Scrolls
>In 1947 the remains of a library belonging to a Hebrew congregation dating from about 125 B.C. to 70 A.D. were found in an area to the west of the Dead Sea known as Khirbet Qumran. Many rolls of papyrus and several of thin-sheet copper were found in several caves. Remnants of more than 600 rolls have been identified in these "Dead Sea Scrolls," most of them of a religious nature.

deckle
>A separate thin wooden frame used to form the border of a hand mold; a curb on either side of the apron to confine the flowing pulp and so determine the width of the paper. The term is also used to describe a torn effect along the edge of a sheet of paper; hence, the natural, untrimmed edge of paper.

deckle edge
>The rough untrimmed edge of paper left by the deckle; also, a rough edge in imitation of this.

decoration
>A picture, design, diagram, etc., which is used to illustrate or explain within the book, or which is used as mere ornamentation, as on the cover or binding of the book.

dedication
>The inscription dedicating the book to a person or cause. In English books of the sixteenth and seventeenth centuries, this is often the only place where the author's name appears.

demotic
>Designating, or pertaining to, a simplified form of the hieratic character, used in Egypt after the 6th or 7th century before Christ, for books, deeds, and other such writings.

**demy**
> A sheet of paper measuring 17 1/2" x 22 1/2"; pertaining to, or made of, any of the sizes of paper called demy; as demy book, demy octavo.

**dentelle**
> A decorative style of binding used during the eighteenth century in France, marked generally by angular or toothed outlines and fine detailed interiors, and emphasizing a lacework border with a center field containing a coat of arms.

**depots litteraires**
> In 1789 all ecclesiastical property in France was put at the disposal of the State, which meant that all the great libraries of the religious foundations, many containing great treasures of manuscripts, became State property. The books were collected in three large depots where they were catalogued and inventoried. After the inventory, the State allowed the heads of the four leading libraries of Paris to select one copy of each book not already in their libraries. The libraries that benefitted from this nationalization were the Bibliotheque Nationale, the Mazarine, the Arsenal, and the Ste-Genevieve.

**descender**
> A descending letter; that is, one which drops below an imaginary line extended across the page (for example, p or q). Also, the stroke of such a letter.

**desiderata (libri desiderati)**
> Something desired as essential or needed; books or manuscripts desired as essential to complete a collection for scholarship.

**devices of printers and publishers**
> Various marks, for example initials, which identified the printer or publisher of a book.

**Dewey Classification System**
> This system of library classification or arrangement divides all knowledge into ten classes, 0-9, each class into a maximum of ten divisions, and each division into a maximum of ten sections.

**Diamond Sutra**
> World's oldest known printed book.

diaper

A bookbinding design in which the cover is ornamented with small figures, often diamond-shaped.

diced

A bookbinding design in which the cover is ornamented with a pattern resembling dice or small squares; checkered.

dictionary arrangement

A combination of the common alphabetical list and the entry-word list. It lists a work in several places, in simultaneous consideration of form and content.

dictionary catalogue

A catalogue of books having the different kinds of entries arranged in a single catalogue.

diplomatics

Properly speaking, the science of medieval documents (diplomata). Its chief concern, at the time of its origin as a special study in the seventeenth century, was with the authenticity of grants held by religious institutions; and it involved, therefore, criticism both of content and of writing. For further reference, see palaeography and sigillography (or spragistics).

diptychs

Wooden or ivory folding tablet books recording memoranda, popular from the first to the seventh centuries A.D. Their covers were highly decorated with designs cut in ivory. They are the earliest examples of exterior book decoration and the direct prototypes of our modern books. They are still in use in the Eastern Church and, in the modern Roman missal, their use is represented by the prayers called Mementos.

direction word

The first word of any page of a book after the first, inserted at the right-hand bottom corner of the preceding page for the assistance of the reader (seldom used in modern printing); also, the word standing at the head of an entry in a dictionary, concordance, etc.; either of the words printed over the first and last columns of a page of a dictionary, encyclopedia, etc., being reprints of the headings of the first and last entries or articles on the page.

**display printing**
Differentiating the arrangement of the lines, as by the use of unequal lengths or different styles or sizes of typefaces; also, the matter thus printed.

**display faces**
Types intended for display as for chapter headings, title pages, etc. (sometimes decorated).

**distribution**
The act of replacing each type in its proper compartment, or box, in the type case.

**diurnal**
A daybook, journal, diary. In earlier times, a daily journal or newspaper.

**doctor blade**
The flexible blade that scrapes ink off a cylinder in photogravure.

**document**
An original or official paper relied upon as the basis of proof or support of something else; also, any writing, book, or other instrument conveying information.

**documentary or cursive hand**
The second style of Greek writing, more natural and rapid, which was used by private individuals for memoranda, letters, documents, etc.

**Donaldson Case**
A petition filed in an English law court in 1775 by Alexander Donaldson, challenging permanent copyright privilege granted to authors, and demanding equal rights for publishers. He won his case.

**Doves Type**
A special printing type designed by Thomas James Cobden-Sanderson and Emery Walker (England) in 1900, for use in their private press--The Doves Press.

**double print**
To produce two images from two negatives in a fixed position on a metal plate.

double-quad crown sheet
   A sheet of paper measuring 40" x 60".

doublure
   The lining of a book cover, especially an unusual one, as one
   of tooled leather, painted vellum, rich brocade, or the like.

dryplate
   A plate, sensitized with an emulsion of silver halide, almost
   invariably in gelatin, although in earlier times in collodion,
   and dried before exposure.

drypoint
   An engraving made with a needle, instead of with burin, and
   differing from an etching in that the plate is engraved without
   the use of acid. The burr, made by the needle is retained,
   not smoothed or polished away as in ordinary engraving; also,
   a print from such an engraving, or the needle with which such
   an engraving is made. Rarely used, because it is easy to destroy
   the beauty of the illustrations produced in this way.

duodecimo
   Size of a book, or of its pages, resulting from folding each
   sheet into twelve leaves, as follows: the original sheet of paper
   is folded into three equal divisions; the parallelogram formed is
   then folded across its shorter diameter and this along its longer
   diameter to form twelve leaves or twenty-four pages with four
   foldings, perpendicular chain lines, the watermark halved at
   the tops of pages three and nine, and two tops and two fronts
   to be cut.

dust jackets
   Also called dust wrappers or book jackets, originally used to
   keep the covers of the books clean.

Dutch printing
   Printing with movable types first took place in Holland. Much
   of the early Dutch printing was done by wandering printers.

# E

edge gilding
>After trimming, the book is squeezed in a press, and the edges are washed with a preparation of red chalk, which tends to enhance the color of the gold that will be placed on them. They are then brushed briskly; size is applied; and the gold is then immediately put on them and, afterwards, burnished.

edges of a book
>foredge, the edge of the book opposite the spine; head, the edge of the book at the top; tail, the edge of the book at the bottom.

edition
>In modern times, edition signifies all the copies of a book printed at any time or times from one setting-up of type. The total number of copies printed without removing the type or plates from the press signifies an impression. A special form of the book in which, for the most part, the original sheets are used, but which differs from the earlier or normal form by the addition of new matter or by some difference in arrangement, is designated an issue.

Editio Princeps
>First edition of a literary work, often in the author's own handwriting.

Egyptian hieroglyphics
>Picture writing (in later times reduced to simpler forms), ordinarily read from the right.

Egyptian language
>The ancient language of Egypt is divided into: Old Egyptian, going back to the First Dynasty; Middle Egyptian, most representative remains being those of the Twelfth Dynasty; Late Egyptian, known best from hieratic writings from the Eighteenth Dynasty to the Twenty-First Dynasty; and demotic Egyptian, extending from the eighth century B.C. to the Christian era.

Einblattdruke
These consist of prints or broadsides, which are commonly
known among bibliographers by their German name. They are
a form of block book which consists, for the most part, of
pictures of a religious character, with or without textual
label or explanation.

electrotype
A means of reproducing a printed surface by making a mold
from the original type form, and depositing in it, by means
of an electric current, a coating of copper which assumes the
form of the original surface in relief. This process renders
a more exact facsimile of the type, but it is costlier than
stereotyping.

Elrod typecasting machine
Casts rules, leads, borders, and plain slugs.

Elston Press
Established by Conwell at New Rochelle, New York, it was
among the first in America to attempt a revival of handpress
methods.

Elyot's Image of Governance
Printed in London in 1541, it is one of the first books with
gold tooling upon it done in England.

Elzevir
Designates books printed by the Elzevirs, a family of seventeenth-
century printers of the Netherlands, and a typeface introduced
by them.

em
Originally, the portion of a line formerly occupied by the letter m, then a square type, used as a unit of measure for
printed matter. It is a space as thick as the type size that it
belongs to is deep: a ten point em is ten points wide. Founders'
spaces are made in nine different thicknesses for each size
of type, and each thickness is based on the thickness of the em.

emblem books
In early times an emblem consisted of a motto expressing a
moral ideal and accompanied by a picture and a short poem

illustrating the idea. A collection of emblems was known as
an emblem book. Emblems and emblem books, in part because
of the development of the art of engraving, were very popular
in all the western European countries in the fifteenth, sixteenth,
and seventeenth centuries.

embroidered bindings
Book bindings done with satin and silk.

en
Half of the width of an em. See em.

Endeavor Type
A 12-point type designed by C. R. Ashbee of England for use
in the Essex House Press, publishers of such notable works
as Cranmer's Psalter (1901), The Prayer Book of King Edward
VII (1903), The Essex House Song Book (1904), and a series of
fourteen Great Poems of the Language.

endpapers
Serve to hide the elements that unite the stitched sections to the
case and to mask the cut edges of the cloth or other substance
used to cover the boards. They contribute little if anything to
the mechanical perfection of the book or to the strength of the
binding.

English type. See point system.

engraving
The act or art of producing, upon hand material, incised or
raised patterns, characters, lines, and the like, especially
in the surface of metal plates or blocks of wood. The practice
of metal engraving in Europe dates from the early Renaissance;
that of wood engraving is earlier, and reached its fullest development in the 15th century.

enlumineurs
Laymen who did illustrations for the manuscripts of the
scriptoria.

entry-word indexes
A subject index usually arranged alphabetically by entry words.

enumerative bibliography
A list of basic reference sources, the tools of research.

epigraph
An inscription on lasting material, as on metal, especially
one on a statue or building.

epigraphy
The study or science of inscriptions, especially the deciphering and interpretation of ancient inscriptions or epigraphs.

epilogue
The concluding section of a book, serving to round out or complete the work.

Epistolae of St. Hieronymus
Printed at Rome, probably by Riessinger (first printer at Naples),
1471; first book issued with a list of gatherings or register.

epistolographic
In paleography, used in writing letters; --applied especially
to the Egyptian demotic characters.

Epitome of Lascaris
Printed at Milan by Paravismus; the first dated book in Greek.

errata
Errors discovered in a book after it has been printed. They are
usually collected and their corrections, printed on a slip or a
page, are pasted into the volume; also called corrigenda.

eschatol
The last page of a codex.

etching
The art of producing pictures or designs by means of etched
plates. In the process, the plate is first covered with varnish
or some other acid-resistant ground, on which the drawing is
scratched with a needle or similar instrument. When the drawing is complete the plate is put into a bath of strong water,
usually dilute nitric acid, and wherever the surface is not
protected by the ground the acid will eat away the metal. When
the ground is then cleaned off with turpentine, the original

design will be seen transferred to the surface of the copper in the form of dull lines--shallow if the acid has been allowed to act for a short time, but broad, deep, and irregular, if the acid has been allowed to "bite" for a longer period.

Eve Binding
A French binding style named after Nicholas Eve, similar to the Fanfare binding, but making use of a central design with corner fleurons, and allowing plenty of leather to show.

Exeter Book
Famous book of Anglo-Saxon poetry written about 970-990.

expansive classification
A library classification system devised by Charles A. Cutter (Newberry Library head librarian) making possible the further development of the Cutter System into seven parallel divisions. Each of the seven divisions is a more detailed expansion of the preceding. A letter notation is used for nonlocal classes, the combinations of letters being arranged alphabetically. A numerical notation is used for geographical subdivisions. Thus F = universal history; F83 = United States History; FE = manners and customs; FE83 = manners and customs in the United States.

"Explicit"
Used at the end of a printed book or manuscript in early times (or at the end of a section of a book or manuscript) to signify the termination.

extract
The title as found on the title page, the edition number if any, and the names of the editor, translator, and illustrator.

# F

Fabriano
> The Italian town where the first paper mill of Christendom was founded about 1270. It is still producing fine papers for general use in printing.

fabric bindings
> Apart from leather and vellum, the most popular material for bindings ever since the medieval period has been fabrics, such as velvet, silk, satin, and canvas. Velvet bindings, plain, embroidered, or occasionally gilt tooled, were very popular during the reign of Elizabeth; and embroidered bindings, usually on satin, reached a high degree of popularity in the 15th century.

fabric printing
> Woodcut or wood-engraved designs, printed on fabric, were used in India and Asia as early as the 4th century B.C.

facsimile edition
> An exact or detailed copy of a manuscript or book or painting.

factotum
> An ornamental block having a space in the center for the insertion of a capital letter of an ordinary font of type in whatever style called for by the text.

fakes
> Among the numerous types are: (1) complete reprints of early books as original editions; (2) imperfect books, "perfected" by the insertion of leaves or parts of leaves, either in facsimile or from another genuine copy from another edition; (3) a book purporting to be a facsimile, which is in fact the invention of the man who printed it.

false hyphen
> The hyphen in two parts of a word which the modern printer has broken between the lines of the printed transcript, especially when that word might be misunderstood as a compound word with a hyphen in the original.

fanfare
>Although the style was developed from the Grolier in the 16th
>century, the name derives from the title of a book published
>two centuries later, <u>Les</u> <u>Fanfares</u> et <u>Courvees</u> <u>Abbadesques</u>.
>As in the Grollier binding, a framework of interlacing bands
>divided the field up into separate compartments; the central
>compartment was filled in, usually, with a stamp representing
>the Crucifixion; and all the spaces formed by the interlacing
>bands were decorated with spiral vines, little sprays of branches,
>and related graceful tooling.

featherweight paper
>Made of esparto grass fiber, which is very light for its bulk.
>It is produced by chopping up the fiber and leaving it half felted
>and full of air. Because it is loose and puffy in texture, it is
>easily cut by binding thread and tends to clog the type during
>printing.

Fell types
>Dr. John Fell, Dean of Christ Church from 1660 to 1686, and
>Bishop of Oxford from 1675 to 1686, in 1667 gave the University
>of Oxford a type foundry, complete with moulds, punches,
>matrices, and several valuable fonts of roman, Saxon, italic,
>and Gothic types of Dutch origin; secured the services of a
>skilled letter founder from Holland; and helped to establish a
>paper mill in nearby Wolvercote.

Fere-Humanistica Type
>A Gothic printing type, round and open, with descenders like
>roman, but with neither the serifs of roman nor the feet of
>Textura. It has been described as "Gothic with roman tenden-
>cies."

fictitious imprint
>One of the methods which is sometimes used to conceal or evade
>a local censor or local copyright law. One form of literary forgery.

filigree bindings
>Bindings with filigree work over gilt metal, and tortoise shell
>with silver or gilt mounts, are found in the work of seventeenth-
>century Spaniards, Germans, and Dutchmen.

filing words
   A synonym for cue and entry words.

fillet
   In bookbinding: an ornamental line, usually of gold, stamped
   or rolled on a book cover, especially at the top and bottom of
   the back; that which completes or fills in the cover design of
   a book after the outline portions are made; a kind of stamp or
   wheel tool with one or more lines, for making fillet lines or
   designs; generally, to bind, furnish, adorn, or make, with or
   as with a fillet. It is seldom if ever used except of leather
   binding and, since about 1700, it has generally been gilded.

Finis
   Found on the last page of a book to mark its conclusion.

finishing
   A final process of the bookbinder's craft, in which the book
   is adorned with designs and lettering.

first book printed in England
   The Dictes or Sayengis of the Philosophres, printed by Caxton
   in 1477. It was translated from the French by his friend and
   patron Anthony Scales. It is the first dated book printed in
   England.

first book printed in the English Language
   Caxton's translation into English of Le Fevre's Le Recueil
   des Histoires de Troye was printed at Bruges in 1474 or
   1475 by Caxton, in association with Mansion, a calligrapher
   who set up the first press in the city.

first edition
   The copies of a work first printed from the same type. These
   are of particular importance to the bibliographer and the
   book collector, because they best reveal what the author really
   intended and wrote.

First Folio
   It was printed by Jaggard in 1623, seven years after Shakespeare's death. It contains all but one of his thirty-seven
   plays, half of which are published for the first time--the
   others having appeared in the Quartos between 1594 and 1622.

55

It is one of the most famous of the rare works of the early seventeenth century.

first printed book
> The Mazarin Bible, better known perhaps as the 42-line Bible (in double columns, 42 lines to a column), was published probably in 1455. It is known as the Mazarine Bible, because the first copy to receive public attention was that housed in the Mazarine Library at Paris. It has also been called, rather inaccurately, the Guttenberg Bible.

fleuron
> A flower-shaped ornament used in bookbinding.

flexible binding
> A book cover made of flexible, rather than rigid, stock.

floated copy
> The reference is to an early, fragile book whose frayed leaves have been mounted by floating the paper on to transparent strengthening material.

flong
> A paper maché sheet, consisting of several layers of paper, superimposed and held together with a special paste. It is laid on the forme in a damp state and beaten down into the type with stiff-haired brushes until it takes the impression of the type to the desired depth. It is then passed through a heated press in which it is dried. When ready, it is trimmed and mounted on a wooden base for printing.

Florentine woodcuts
> A form practiced in Florence, Italy, during the 15th century, characterized by a combination of black-and-white line passages within the same cut.

flyleaf
> A blank leaf at the beginning or end of a book, circular, or program; the half portion of the endpaper next to the work proper.

fly sheet
> A small loose advertising sheet, a single-page or double-page

leaflet, smaller than a broadside or broadsheet, which is printed
for distribution broadcast; also, a sheet of a folder, booklet,
or catalogue giving instructions or information regarding material which follows.

fly's type
A two-point type; that is, about the height of the space between
the printed lines in the average book.

fly title
A leaf which introduces a certain part of the book, by title,
brief description, or legend; a cross between a half title and
a divisional title. In England, a bastard title.

fold format
The number of times a sheet of paper which is used in printing
a book is folded in order to produce the page size desired.
See format.

Folger Library
Has an endowment of over ten million dollars and the largest
collection of Shakespeareana in the world, containing over 200
original folios.

foliation
The numbering of the leaves, commonly placed at the head of
the paper, similar to today's paging. Caxton foliated a few books
from 1483 on, but the practice was not common until the last
five or six years of the 15th century, and seems to have been
more usual in Missals and other service books. The earliest
form was the word or abbreviation for folio, followed by a roman
numeral. In time, the roman numeral gave place to an arabic
number. By 1570-1580, the arabic number stood alone, leaving
foliation limited to use in legal works or works of an antiquarian
character.

folio
Formed of sheets each folded once, making two leaves or four
pages; as, a folio edition, a work in five-folio volumes. In
book work, the folio was the largest size ordinarily used. Three
or four sheets were generally placed together in one gathering
of six to eight leaves and sewn through in binding. In a folio the

chain marks are perpendicular and the watermark is in the
middle of the first leaf. Most of Caxton's books are folios.

folioing
Used in place of the word foliating, to number the leaves,
rather than the pages. On old manuscripts, more than one
foliation is often found. The British Museum's foliation, which
is always in the right-hand corner of the rectos, should be
used.

foolscap
Paper in sheets measuring 13 x 16 (or 13 x 17); so called from
the watermark of a fool's cap and bells used by old paper makers.

forage
Corruption of fore edge; hence, the front edge of a book which
was often decorated or lettered.

Force Collection
The Peter Force Collection, consisting of 60,000 volumes of
Americana--books, early newspapers, maps, MSS., incunabula,
and other material, was purchased by Congress in 1867 for
$100,000.

fore-edge decoration
The fore edges of books were often gold-tooled, gauffered,
and even painted, especially in Venice, but occasionally also
in France and England. When the medieval method of shelving
books with their backs toward the wall ceased, and the modern
method began, the practice was discontinued.

forels
Book covers made of leather, charmingly chased and often
bearing heraldic ornamentation. They were made in the fifteenth
and sixteenth centuries, especially in Italy, and were in the
form of "slip off" cases.

format
Generally, the form, size, and style or makeup of a publication.

form concept
Designates the type and nature of a publication, as opposed to
its content; also used to refer to classes of literature.

Specifically, the term describes the book relative to the manner in which the original sheet is folded. Since it does not
indicate the size of the original sheet, format as such does not
signify size.

forme
The actual unit of printing laid on the foundation of the press,
over which flat pieces of wood are laid and then hammered,
so that any pieces of type which have been raised by the pressure are made level with the rest of the type. Also expressed
as form.

formschneider
Guilds of professional woodcutters.

Forty Line Bible
Between 1448 and 1460 a number of works were printed at Mainz.
Among them was an uncompleted Forty Line Bible printed in
double columns.

Forty-two Line Bible
Planned by Gutenberg and probably begun by him, but apparently completed by Fust and Schoeffer after they had severed their
connection with Gutenberg. A few of the forty-five known surviving copies contain on certain leaves headings printed in red,
and are therefore the earliest examples of color printing.

forty-eightmo
A method of folding which produces sheets or gatherings of
forty-eight leaves.

forwarding
Includes all those functions of the binder which are necessary
to secure the pages and cover: collating the sheets, sewing them
together to bands, and fastening them securely to covers or
boards.

foul case
The presence, in the divisions of the case, of letters which
do not belong there.

founders' type
A metal block of six surfaces. The belly (front side) contains

horizontal furrows (nicks) which indicate position of type and
identification. The back, opposite the belly, is blank. One side
is also blank, while the other contains the pin-mark. The upper
end (face) contains the molded letter.

foundry
An establishment in which fonts are cast.

fount
Also font. An assortment of type of one size and style, including the conventional proportion of all the letters in the
alphabet, large and small, as well as punctuation marks,
figures, accents, etc. Generally spelled font in America and
fount in England.

Fourdrinier Machine
A power driven papermaking machine on which paper was
formed by means of an endless moving band of wire mesh,
upon which the fibers could be interlocked, and through which
the surplus water might be drained in much the same manner
as in the hand mould. Patented in 1798 by Nicholas-Louis
Robert, an inspector in a paper mill owned by François Didot.

Fragment of the Last Judgment
One of the earliest concrete evidence of printing at Mainz.
Discovered in an old binding at Mainz in 1892; its estimated
date of printing is 1444-1445.

Fraktur Type
A kind of Bastarda Type with spiky, pointed narrow letters,
which became popular in the early part of the 16th century.
It is sometimes called Broken Type.

frames
Supports around the printing area at the level of the type. When
not level with the printing surfaces of the type, they are a
source of printing failure in stereotyping.

Frankfurt Messkataloge
The term refers to the early trade catalogs composed by book
dealers and distributed at fairs in Germany beginning in 1564,
at first in the city of Frankfurt and later in Leipzig.

**French blind tooled bindings**
One of the main, although not exclusive, characteristic is
perpendicular lines; another is the use of panel stamps.

**French joint**
Consists in leaving about one-eighth of an inch between the
edge of the front cover and the back, which gives the leather
a space in which to bend when the book is opened.

**frisket**
Originally, a light frame to hold the sheet of paper to the tympan
in printing on a hand press; now, also, a sheet stretched in a
frame with parts cut out to lay an inked form, so that only certain parts shall be printed.

**frontispiece**
An ornamental figure or illustration fronting the first page or
title page of a book; formerly, the title page itself.

**fugitive literature**
Literature that deals with matters of temporary interest.

**full standard description**
Aims at laying the book fully before the researcher, so far as it
can be done without reprinting the text or photographing the
leaves. It may include discussion of the notes on the text of
a book, or references to the engraving plates.

**furniture**
Pieces of wood or metal, smaller in height than the type, which
are placed between or around pages or other matter in a form,
serving to give proper blank spaces and (with quoins) to lock up
and justify the matter.

# G

galley

A long, shallow tray with edges on three sides, somewhat lower
than the height of the type. Galleys are made in a variety of
sizes for different purposes, a book galley being about two feet
long and six to eight inches wide and a bit more than half an
inch deep. Each stickful of type is placed on the galley as it is
completed, until there is a long slab of type. In early times
the galley was one-page long. Today it contains three or more
pages.

galley or slip proof

When there is sufficient type on the galley, a piece of metal
furniture is set against the last line to prevent it from falling
over, and a long strip of wooden furniture is placed down the
entire length of the free edge. Between this strip and the side
of the galley, wedges are inserted and tightened up so that a
firm pressure is applied to every line. The galley is now placed
on the proofing press, inked, and printed on to a long strip of
paper. This is the galley or slip proof. Correction in galley
is easier than correction in page form.

galvanic battery

One way of making a hard printing plate. The mold from the
type is made in wax, impregnated or carefully dusted with
black lead; it is then placed into a galvanic bath, where a
strong metallic deposit is laid over it, and the deposit is afterwards backed up with alloy.

Garamond Type

Thought to have been designed by Claude Garamond at Paris
in the sixteenth century, but actually cut a century later by
Jean Jannon. There are many versions of the Jannon Garamond
type. The italic is unusual in the variation of angle and the
free sweep of the kerned letters; the capitals show two or
three distinct slopes; and the erratic capitals join pleasingly
with the erratic lowercase.

garter
> The band around the base of a hand press.

gathering
> The leaves of a book collectively that are folded and stitched into one quire or signature; also, the act of collecting, by hand or machine, the printed and folded sections or sheets in the order in which they are to be bound.

gauffered edges
> The edges of books which were gilded and had designs impressed on them with ordinary binding tools. They are found in abundance in French, German, and Italian works of the 16th and 17th centuries.

genealogy
> The science that deals with family histories and their bibliographies.

general bibliographies
> Lists which deal with a variety of subjects and authors and may include several languages and many disciplines of knowledge.

gesso
> A plaster-like material (plaster of Paris, gypsum), for use in painting or in making, for example, bas-reliefs. It was applied to oriental pasteboard bindings in the 17th, 18th, and 19th centuries.

gift-books
> Literary collections, published often under sentimental titles, which are intended primarily for souvenir gifts or keepsakes.

gilt tooling
> Introduced in Venice by the Moors. Sheets of finely beaten gold leaf were laid on the leather, and the design was impressed on it by means of heated tools of different patterns.

girts
> Leather straps tied around the barrel of a hand printing press.

glaire
> After the design is blinded in, the material is treated with glaire, a preparation of egg albumen that provides a base for holding the gold to the surface. Gold leaf is then laid on and the heated tool impressed again, through it, into the blind impression.

gloss
> A brief explanation or a translation or definition, sometimes appearing in the margin, between the lines of a text, or in a workbook based upon the text. (The word is, in modern times, often used pejoratively, as when "to gloss" a passage means to misinterpret it, and "to gloss over" a passage means to "explain away" or excuse.) Glossaries developed from the custom of collecting glosses into lists.

gluing up
> The application of the glue into the back or spine of the sewn gathering in order to produce a rounded back.

goatskin
> The finest of all leathers for binding. It is called morocco, from the land of its origin. "Levant morocco" is still used to designate the finest skins. Goatskins were used in ancient bindings, perhaps earlier than even vellum.

goffered. See gauffered edges.

gold tooling
> A stamp is impressed in blind on the leather, and the impression is painted over with the glaire of egg (albumen). When the albumen is dry, it is in turn painted over with palm or cocoanut oil, on which a piece of gold leaf is placed, and a stamp, heated to the proper temperature, is carefully reimpressed in exactly the same place as originally. Introduced into Europe in the sixteenth century, gold tooling was especially popular in Italy and Spain.

Golden Cockerel Press
> A modern private press dedicated to printing first-class editions of books of merit.

Golden Type
> A 14-point roman based upon an early font used by Nicholas

Jenson. It was one of three types designed by William Morris for use by The Kelmscott Press, which he founded in 1891.

Gothic Minuscule
A development in the 12th century of the tendency, on the part of French, German, and English scribes of the 10th and 11th centuries, to compress their lettering in order to save space. The hand consisted of long, angular, pointed letters, also called the Carolingian Minuscule, and was the form on which most of the early European printers based their first types. The four common Gothic types are: Textura, Fere-Humanistica, Rotunda, and Bastarda.

Gothic-Roman Transitional Types
A mixture of Fere-Humanistica and roman types, in which neither truly predominated. They were in use before the advent of roman types proper. Other transitional types were generally part Gothic and part roman.

gouge
Binding tools are similar to pieces of type, save that they have longer shanks and are made of brass instead of lead; they are set in wooden handles. With the gouge, curved lines are made.

graffiti
Rudely scratched drawings or inscriptions, found on rocks, walls, vases, and other objects.

Grammatica Brevis
The first book to contain secular music. It was produced at Venice by Theodorus.

Granjon Type
Produced in 1924 by George W. Jones for the Linotype. A popular printing type, it has been described as "a true Garamond design," clear, clean, dignified, timeless.

graphology
A psuedo-science which purports to relate individual writing differences to those of, for example, nation, sex, and profession.

graver
>A cutting or shaving tool, as an engraver's burin.

Grecs du Roi
>Three Greek types, based upon the handwriting of the callig-
>rapher Angelos Vergetios, which were produced by Claude
>Garamonde, one of the earliest and most distinguished of all
>French type designers. They are deemed unique for their
>"evenness of color, precision of casting, and exactness of
>alignment and justification."

Greek alphabets
>As found in early inscriptions, Greek alphabets have been
>classified as Eastern and Western. From the former derives
>the alphabet of the manuscript; from the latter derives the
>Latin alphabet.

Greek type
>Type cut in the Greek alphabet for use in reproducing Greek
>texts and for reproduction of Greek words. The Greek type
>which is the basis of most later printing in Greek was designed
>by Aldus Manutius, who began printing in 1494.

Gregnog Press
>A modern private press which was established primarily for
>the purpose of printing good editions of works of the writers
>of Wales.

Grolier Library
>One of the outstanding libraries of fine bindings, composed
>of rare leathers gold-tooled in geometric designs. The library
>was sold and widely scattered in the seventeenth century but
>some 400 bindings are known to have survived into the twentieth
>century. Most have a pattern of interlacing bars, bands, or rib-
>bons with delicate scrolls of slender gold line.

Grolier List
>Published by the Grolier Club of New York (named after the
>French bibliophile of the 16th century), it is regarded as a
>standard by book collectors. It is significant, in other words,
>to possess an item which is contained in a Grolier catalogue or
>bibliographical publication.

## Gros Paragon Type
Of the three founts of Grecs du Roi types produced by Garamonde, the Gros Parangon was the largest in size; it was first used in Estienne's folio New Testament, published in 1550.

## Gros Romain Type
Of the three founts of Grecs du Roi types produced by Garamonde, the Gros Romain type, medium in size, was the first to be used, appearing in an edition of Eusebius' Ecclesiastical History, published by Robert Estienne in 1544.

## Grotesque Alphabet
A strange block book of twenty-four pages, no complete copies of which survive, which contains pictures of the letters of the alphabet made up from human forms. It is an eminent example of the block book in that it surpasses all others in conception, drawing, and engraving.

## guarding
In bookbinding, a slip or strip of strong, thick, flexible material and bank-note paper or linen, which is inserted between the leaves at the back, to hold the thread which otherwise would cut the paper.

## guide-letter
A blank space left by the printer to indicate where the capital or large decorative letter, at the beginning of the chapter, should be placed.

## guillotine
A machine used to trim the edges of a book. It has three knives and is capable of making three cuts in rapid succession. The books are placed under a clamp and the first knife descends to cut the foredge; as it withdraws, the two other knives come down at right angles to cut the head and the tail.

## guillotined
Describes the edges of paper in a book which are clearly cut.

## Gulden Spiel, Das
The illustrated edition printed by Zainer in 1472 contains striking woodcuts of the seven deadly sins.

gum arabic
> Used in the manufacture of adhesives, inks, etc., and in textile printing. Parts of a printing plate which are not to receive ink are often painted over with a solution of gum arabic.

Gutenberg developments
> Three printing inventions were completed by him in 1445, namely: (1) the press itself, making possible printing on both sides of a sheet; (2) the adjustable type-mould for casting separate alphabetical letters, large or small, in accurate alignment; and (3) the viscous ink required by metallic printing surfaces.

# H

half binding
> A strip of leather which is glued to the bands of a book to protect the threads which cover the bands.

half sheet
> One-half of a sheet of paper which has not been folded, used for printing maps and similar materials.

half stuff
> The material which results from the processing of wood pulps, in which the individual fibers have been separated by breakers.

half title
> A sheet of paper which precedes the title page, which may carry the book's short title on the recto side and the printer's imprint on the verso side, and exists mainly to keep the title page clean and to identify the book to which the first sheet belongs, something a blank first leaf does not.

halftone
A photo-mechanical relief method, invented by George Meisenbach in 1881, which is used in modern illustration. The negative
form of the original design is made on the photographic plate as
a series of transparent dots, by the use of a special kind of
screen. The breaking up of the continuous tones of the original
design into a mass of minute individual dots, when printed,
gives back an optical illusion of continuous tone. The dots are
equally spaced but of varying sizes. The effect of a light tone
is given by very small dots; the darker tones are made possible
by the use of larger and larger dots, up to a solid black.

half uncial
A book hand formed by combining uncial characters with carefully written cursive forms. It is the typical book hand from
the earliest times in Ireland, and from the 7th century to the
Norman Conquest in England.

hand composition
The monotype and linotype machines have made possible the
incredible speed in casting and setting type characteristic of
modern printing. Much composition, however, is still done
by hand: correction of galley and page proofs; title page and
chapter headings imposition; initial letters or decorative units
not available for machine composition.

hand letter
In binding, a letter of brass or foundry type used in a pallet
by a finisher.

hand lettering
The earliest works in western hand lettering were written
entirely in capitals, as is evident from the inscriptions cut on
ancient monuments. In the 7th and 8th centuries, however, hand
lettering began to assume national characteristics; in France
we identify the Merovingian style; in Italy, the Lombardic; and
in Spain, the Visigothic.

hand-made paper
Has strength in two directions and can therefore be folded
in any way.

hand press
The earliest form of printing press, used from the last quarter
of the 15th century to 1800. Typesetting, typecasting, distribution, and all other operations were done by hand. It was built
within an upright frame constructed from stout timber and required nine principal steps to operate: (1) preparation of the
ink balls; (2) inking of the form; (3) laying the paper; (4) folding
the tympan; (5) setting the rounce; (6) pulling the impression;
(7) returning the plank; (8) opening the tympan; (9) removing
the printed sheet.

handwriting
All manuscripts of the earlier periods prior to the Restoration
were handwritten. (Descriptions of the various forms and styles
are made under the proper alphabetical listing.)

Harleian Bindings
Bindings done by Thomas Eliott and Christopher Chapman for
Robert Harley, First Earl of Oxford. They were usually tooled
on red morocco, decorated with a broad outer border enclosing
a richly tooled oval or lozenge-shaped centerpiece.

Harleian Manuscripts
That portion of the great library collected by Robert and Edward
Harley, first and second Earls of Oxford, which were sold to
Parliament in 1753 by the second Countess and her daughter
the Duchess of Portland for the low price of 10,000 pounds.
They form a part of the foundation collection of The British
Museum. Among the Harleian Manuscripts are: the Winchester
Psalter, excellent copies of the Canterbury Tales, an illuminated
copy of Gower's Confessio Amantis, and an early copy of Cicero's
Paradoxa.

headband
Bookbinding; narrow strip of cloth sewn or glued by hand to a
book at the extreme ends of a book's backbone. Printing: a thin
iron slip at the top of the tympan.

headline, page
May appear on both the left- and right-hand pages, or left- or
right-hand page, or may appear in part on both. Ideally, it should
be an invaluable part of the system of reference, directing the
reader efficiently to the place which he is looking for. Too often,
however, it is at best decorative only, serving no practical end.

headline, running
The title of the book which appears either on both the left and the right sides of the page, or on the left side only, in which instance the right side has a section headline. Also called title headline.

headline, section
A partial book title, or any subdivision title (for example, a chapter title).

head margin. See margin.

head of press
The cheeks of the hand press are joined by four cross pieces. The upper one, called the cap, serves to keep the cheeks apart. The one below it is called the head.

head ornament. See headpieces.

headpieces
Any engraved ornaments at the head of a chapter or page. They are generally small and nearly always narrow horizontal bands. They may incorporate the lettering of the chapter head or provide an island space in which to print it.

height-to-paper
A piece of type has three dimensions, the longest of which represents the distance from the surface of the press, on which the type rests, to the surface of the paper that is to be printed. This dimension, known as height-to-paper, is the same for all sizes of type, the large capitals at the top of a poster or the small type used in footnotes.

Helgen (picture prints)
Simple block-like pictures from woodcut or wood engraved designs which have little if any shading. Most were pictures of saints.

helioengraving
A photomechanical process producing a photogelatin plate for printing; the plate so made; also, a print made from such a plate.

heliography
>An early photographic process which is still used in photoen-
>graving. A polished metal plate, coated with a preparation of
>asphalt, is exposed under a design or in a camera and then
>treated with a suitable solvent. The light renders insoluble
>those parts of the film which it strikes, whereupon a permanent
>image is formed, which can be etched upon the plate by the use
>of acid. (Also, the description of the sun, corresponding to
>geography.)

Heliogravure
>The process of making almost exact reproductions of line en-
>gravings through the use of a photographic negative. From the
>plates produced in this way, prints are made.

hell box
>The container which is set aside in printing houses for the
>reception of defective or battered types. These are resold to
>the founder as scrap metal; hence the name.

Hereford Cathedral
>In medieval libraries many of the books were kept chained, in
>the Laurentian Library at Florence, for instance, in beautifully
>carved shelves. The Hereford Cathedral is one of the best
>examples of a chained library in England.

Hiberno-Saxon hand
>A medieval style of writing in which the calligraphist and scholar-
>poet Alcuin was trained. Many magnificent examples of the style
>are still extant, notably the Book of Kells and the Gospels of
>Lindisfarne.

hieratic
>A cursive form of ancient Egyptian writing, simpler than the
>hieroglyphics, which is found in documentary, literary, and
>scientific papyri. It was used most generally by priests. The
>oldest dated papyrus, the Papyrus Prisse, is written in hieratic.

hieroglyphic
>Picture writing of the ancient Egyptian, containing characters
>of two main classes: (1) ideographic, in which each character
>represents either the object itself or a symbol associated with
>it (for example, the ostrich feather as a symbol of truth);

(2) phonetic, in which each character represents either an alphabetic sound (for example, the hawk·representing the sound a) or a complete syllable.

historiated
Adorned with figures which have significance, such as flowers, animals, as distinguished from scrolls, diapers, etc.; used of initials, capitals, or borders in manuscripts or early books.

historical bibliography
Deals with the history of book production; that is, the history of writing, printing, binding, illustrating, publishing.

hollow back
The back of a book cover which is not fastened to the bound backs of the sections. Most modern books are bound with hollow backs. A hollow back is best recognized by opening the book to the full and noting if the back is separated.

holograph
A manuscript written wholly in the handwriting of the author.

Homereion
The name for the main hall of a library, based on the practice of Greek librarians of having a statue or bust of Homer on display.

Homiliae
In the Homiliae of Chrisostomus, printed by Lauer at Rome, page numbers (arabic numerals) were first used; they were placed at the top of the page.

hornbook
A kind of primer common in England from the sixteenth to the eighteenth centuries. A sheet of vellum was mounted on wood and covered (for protection) by horn (hence hornbook). The alphabet and the Lord's Prayer are the commonest letterings upon them, always beginning with a cross. The sheet of transparent horn was kept in place by strips of brass fastened with nails having facetted tops.

Horrea Charataria
A government warehouse for storing papyrus.

hose
> An oblong block of wood which guided and stabilized the vertical motion of the spindle or screw of the hand press; to the bottom of it was hung the platen, a piece of mahogany four inches thick, on the top of which was fixed a small steel center hole in which the toe of the screw worked.

humanistic or Neo-Carolingian script
> A revival of classical lettering as opposed to Gothic lettering.

human leather binding
> The use of human skin for bookbinding is not unknown. It is said that a friend of the French writer Camille Falmmarion bequeathed her skin to him. Flammarion had the skin tanned and used it to bind one of his own books. A copy of the constitution of 1793, now in the Carravalet Library at Paris, is bound in the skin of one of the revolutionaries who was killed at the time.

Huntington Library
> Unique among the libraries of America in that it is the only one that can rival the European and ancient libraries in the fields of incunabula and manuscripts. It posses over 5,000 incunabula, an extensive collection of manuscripts, and is also strong in American history, English literature, and other fields. Among the special collections are: the Gundulf Bible, the Ellesmere Chaucer, one of the most important texts of the Canterbury Tales; the MS. autobiography of Benjamin Franklin.

hydraulic press
> A press which is operated by liquid which is forced through a small oriface.

hygroscopic
> Readily taking up and retaining moisture--a property of parchment.

Hypnerotomachia Poliphili
> The only illustrated book printed by Aldus, notable because it is perhaps the finest example, among Italian incunabula, of printing harmonized with woodcut illustration.

74

# I

iconography
   The art of representation by pictures or images; the description
   or study of portraiture or representation.

ideal copy
   A book which is complete, that is, has all of its leaves exactly as it left the printer's shop: is in that state considered to
   represent the final and most perfect state of the book.

ideal entry
   One that is exact, clean, terse, and perfectly appropriate.

ideogram
   A picture or pictorial symbol, an early form of hieroglyphic
   which, expressing no sound, symbolizes directly the idea of
   the thing and not the name of it. Modern examples are: the
   hand or arrow pointing direction; the barber pole of red and
   white stripes; the Indian in front of the cigar store. Ideograms
   precede phonograms in the development of writing.

illuminated manuscript
   A decorated manuscript (a letter or part of a page) with gold
   or silver or brilliant colors, or with elaborate designs and
   miniature pictures.

illumination
   The act of adorning, as an initial letter or a word, with flour-
   ishes and designs in gold, brilliant colors, etc.; a book or page,
   with borders, initial letters, or miniature pictures in colors and
   gold, as in manuscripts of the Middle Ages.

illustrations in books
   Intended primarily to elucidate the text or to place the reader
   in a better position for visualizing the events narrated.

imposition
   The process of arranging the type pages in the proper position,
   with relation to one another, and then wedging them firmly in

a frame (called a chase), so that neither the inking nor the pressure exerted by the press will disturb the alignment of types or mar the correct sequence of pages, when the sheet is folded in a particular manner.

impression
The whole number of copies printed at one time, that is, the total number of copies, in ordinary circumstances, which are printed without removing the type or plates from the press; loosely, the pressure of type forms or plates on the paper in a printing press. See reprint.

imprimatur
A license or approval, granted by secular or ecclesiastical authority, to print or publish a book, paper, etc.

Imprimerie Royale
The French press founded in 1640 by Louis XIV.

imprint
The publisher's name, place of publication, date, and information regarding the person by or for whom the book was printed, generally found on the lower part of the title page. In library cataloguing, the copyright date is generally considered part of the imprint. When this information appears at the end of the book, it is called the colophon.

incipit
In the late Middle Ages it was common for a scribe to begin his manuscript with a paragraph, now called the incipit, in which he named the author, the text, and occasionally himself, the place, and the date.

incised lines
Cut-in, carved, or engraved lines which form a design on a stamp or pottery. Stamps were commonly used in the decorative arts even in the late Middle Ages.

incunabulist
One who makes a study of early books (cradle books or fifteeners), that is, those printed before the sixteenth century.

incunabulum
A book printed before 1500 A.D. Since the first printed books
resemble the medieval manuscript in size, form, and appearance, they are exceptionally large and ornate and, as
examples of early printing, are prized by modern collectors.
The existing incunabula, large in number, include about 360
which were printed in England, among the most famous being
Caxton's edition of Chaucer's Canterbury Tales and Le Morte
d'Arthur of Malory.

index
A table or list, usually alphabetical, of topics, names, etc.,
in a book (or treatise, for example), giving the number of the
page or pages where each subject is treated, commonly placed
at the end of the work; also a list of periodicals or books, or
a guide to them (for example, a periodical index, a book index).

Index Society
Founded in England in 1878.

india gum
A commercial variety of gum arabic.

india paper
A very thin and strong type of rag paper first used in England
in the mid-nineteenth century; used today primarily for private
printings.

ingots
Slugs melted down after printing to be used again in the linotype machine.

initials
Large capital letters, woodcuts or metal casings, used at
the beginning of a chapter or paragraph. Also called ornamental
initials.

ink
Writing ink is a liquid made of oak-gall and water; it turns
brown with age. It was used, however, by early typographers.
Printing ink is a paint made of linseed oil and lamp black; it
was recognized early by the pioneers of movable type as the
only suitable medium.

inlay
>Inlaying of different colors of leather is another method of design; it is occasionally used in conjunction with blind or gold tooling or both.

inscribed copy
>Autographed by author, usually to or for someone.

inserts
>Type matter or illustrations which are not printed in regular sections, but are tipped in later between the pages.

Institut International de Bibliographie
>Founded at Brussels in 1895, its chief task is to create a world bibliography and, toward that end, it has affiliated itself with several national societies.

intaglio
>An engraving or incised figure in stone or other hard material; specifically, a figure or design which is incised in the block or plate, inked, and then wiped; the impression is made by strong pressure, so that the paper is forced into the incisions, which alone is inked.

intaglio printing
>Printing done from an engraved or intaglio surface, instead of from a design in relief.

intagliotype
>A process for producing, from a design drawn on a coated metal plate, an intaglio plate for printing; also, a print from such a plate. (Line engraving, dry-point, etching, stipple, messotint, aquatint, and photogravure are different methods of intaglio illustration.)

interleave
>To insert a leaf or leaves in; to bind with blank leaves inserted between the others, as a book.

International Copyright
>By the International Copyright of 1838, works first published in foreign countries, and foreign works first published in the British Empire, were granted copyright protection upon regis-

tration of the title and the deposit of one ordinary edition copy
of the book at Stationers' Hall for delivery to the British Museum.

interlibrary cooperation
The Scandinavian countries appear to have carried the idea of
library cooperation further than most countries in that they
have a formal plan of international, interlibrary cooperation
on special and research library levels.

interlibrary loan
Not unknown in the Middle Ages. Books were lent to be copied
and even to be read, sometimes between libraries as far apart
as France and Greece or England and Austria. The Library
of Congress and Harvard University, to mention just two, have,
from time to time, placed certain restrictions on loans. The
photostat copy is a good substitute for direct loans, and the
largest libraries in the world constantly render service to other
libraries, as well as to individual scholars, by arranging to
have photostatic or photographic copies made of single pages,
articles, and even whole books and manuscripts, provided
copyright is not involved.

Intertype
Similar to the Linotype, it has an automatic centering and
quadding device, and an attachment for hand-composing lines
in large-type sizes. It is considered an improvement over the
Linotype in that its system of standardization permits improvements which the manufacturers may introduce to be incorporated with machines already in the printer's office.

invention of printing with movable type
Generally credited to Gutenberg, who lived in Germany between
1398 and 1468.

Irish Binding
Early Irish manuscripts were generally bound in simple limp
leather covers. They were kept in book boxes or "Cumdachs"
and are today of extraordinary interest. One of the finest is the
Stowe Missal, dating from about the eleventh century. It is now
deposited in the museum of the Royal Irish Academy.

issue
A special form of a book in which, for the most part, the original

printed sheets are used; but the book differs from an earlier form by the addition of new matter or by some difference in arrangement.

Italian Hand
Imported from Italy during the seventeenth century, it eventually supplanted the English hand.

Italian printers, earliest
The first printers in Italy were Conrad Sweynheym and Arnold Ponnartz, two Germans from Mainz.

Italic Type
Now used chiefly for emphasis in a main body of roman text, it was originally a body type in its own right, introduced by Aldus Manutius of Venice in 1501. It is supposedly based on the handwriting of Petrarch, but probably derives from one of the many forms of the Humanistic hand, which was the manuscript hand used around 1500 in the Papal Chancery for briefs and informal documents.

ivory bindings
Carvings of ivory had an important role in early bindings. Apart from diptychs, the earliest known decorative binding consists of plaques of ivory carved with biblical scenes, a centered lamb within a wreath of cloisonne work, with inlays of colored glass.

# J

jade books
Early Chinese books exist which are made of leaves of jade, with inscriptions in the decorative Chinese character, run in with gold.

Jansenist Binding
   A simple style of binding developed in France, in the latter
   part of the seventeenth century, in which a centerpiece is
   repeated in each of the four corners, the rest of the surface
   being left undecorated.

Japanese Vellum
   A fine, strong paper made of Japanese shrubs, notably the
   Broussonetia. It is characterized by a creamy tint and smooth
   surface, as is Vellum, and is much used for engravings.

japanning
   Covering with a coat of hard brilliant varnish; giving, in this
   way for example, a glossy black to leather.

jet
   A projection at the bottom of a piece of foundry mold which is
   planed off in finishing; also called tail or tanq.

Joanna Type
   One of the interesting types designed by Eric Gill, an outstanding type designer of the early 20th century.

joiner
   A worker in wood who does lighter and more ornamental work
   than that of the carpenter; also a woodworking machine, as
   for sawing, planing, mortising, tenoning, grooving, etc.

joint
   The longtitudinal ridge on either outer side of the backbone
   of the book, the grooves where the cover hinges; also, re-
   inforcing strip, as of muslin, around end sections and end
   leaves.

journeyman
   A worker who has learned a handicraft or trade, distinguished
   from an apprentice, foreman, or master.

justifying
   The process of arranging letters and spaces so that the right-
   hand margin of the page will be even. Early printers, among
   other means, used variations of spelling to aid them to justify
   lines.

# K

## Keepsake, The
Published by Charles Heath, 1827-1857, it started the fashion in England of small books illustrated with delicate engravings on steel.

## Kelmscott Press
The founding of the Kelmscott Press by William Morris in 1891 is said to mark the beginning of the private press movement.

## kern
A part of the face of a type which projects beyond the body or shank, as in an italic f or j.

## King's Font
One of three printing types designed by Charles Ricketts for use in his press, The Vale Press (founded in 1896).

## Koran
The first major item of written literature among the Moslems, a collection of the sayings of the Prophet Mohammed brought together by his followers; it now comprises both the Bible and the philosophic base of Mohammedanism.

## Korean woodcut
They are always in outline, thickened here and there, in character different from early European work of the same sort, but far better than it in drawing and execution. Most of the blocks from which Korean prints are made are of soft wood, not box, and are cut with a short knife of unusual form set in a handle.

# L

label title pages

The earliest example of a printed title is found in a Papal Bull of Pius II, printed by Fust and Schoeffer in 1463. It is very brief and gives the name of the author and the title only. Similar title pages, containing only a brief "label" title near the top of an otherwise blank page, came to be known as label title pages.

label titles with printers' devices

The colophon originally appeared at the back of the book, but gradually was transferred to the title page. The printer's device was the first item from the colophon to be transferred to the title page, where it began to replace the woodcut illustration immediately below the label title.

label titles with woodcut pictures

Label titles were often printed from wood blocks as well as with movable types. It was inevitable, therefore, that title pages would be produced with label titles at the top of the page and woodcut illustrations below. Early examples of such title pages are found in Tynson's Lydgate Testament (1515) and Abraham Vele's Deceyte of Women (c. 1550).

lacuna (lacunae)

A blank space or hiatus, as in a manuscript; a part which should be filled by desiderati to complete the collection or period.

laid lines

A mark left on the finished paper by the wires which constitute the bottom of the paper mold. They are in the form of translucent lines running across the sheet, close together in one direction and about an inch apart in the other.

laid mold

That type of mold-making paper which consists of a close mesh of fine wires (fibers of the pulp) that run lengthwise and cross at intervals of about three-fourths of an inch, where they meet coarser wires (fibers). Until the 19th century, all paper was produced in this manner.

laid paper
A hand manufactured paper, made in laid molds.

lampblack
A substance used in paints, varnishes, and printer's ink.

large folio. See crown sheet.

large paper
Larger and finer paper, used for special and more expensive copies.

Lasteyrie
A monumental bibliography of French historical and archaeological societies.

later cursive hand
One of the five handwriting styles practiced during the Roman period, the 2nd to the 8th century A.D. The first was the Quadrata or Square Capital hand; the second was the Rustic Capital hand; the third was the Uncial hand; the fourth, the Later Cursive hand; and the last, the Half Uncial hand. The Later Cursive hand had two main characteristics: ligatures and the uneven height of its letters.

Latin alphabet
The earliest Greek settlement in Italy was the colony of Cumae, now the Bay of Naples. From this focus the Greek culture radiated to the aboriginal races of Italy. Among the most valuable properties of these people was a script alphabet for the writing of books. From this alphabet, called by modern writers Pelasgic, all the subsequent Latin (Italian) alphabets derive.

Laws of Solon
The earliest legislation of the Greeks; preserved on wooden planks.

layer
The person who separates the sheets of paper from the felt and stacks them.

lay of case
> The manner in which type is distributed among the boxes of the pair of cases; standard through the English-speaking world.

layout
> The preparatory makeup of a work: the type or types to be used; the number of lines to the page; the length of lines; illustrations, if any, etc.

lead
> The thin strip of type metal used to separate lines of type in printing. It is as long as the line is wide and varies in thickness, being 1, 1 1/2, 2, 3, and 4 points. Leads which are six and twelve points thick or more are called clumps.

leaf
> A sheet of paper, usually in a book, having a page on each side.

leather binding
> Until very recently, the materials for book covers have consisted exclusively of leather; nor has any textile of equal flexibility, toughness, and durability yet been found to take its place. The leathers for bookbinding come from the pig, the calf, the goat, the sheep, and the seal.

Le Gascon Binding
> A seventeenth-century modification of the fanfare binding (made by a French binder who has been called Le Gascon) with dotted scrolls and ornaments instead of unbroken ones, a style termed pointillé. Le Gascon bindings are chronologically divided into three styles: the earliest, in which the binder combined strapwork and decoration with normal tools; a later manner, in which he introduced a certain amount of pointillé tooling in the corners and centerpiece designs; the latest style, in which he tooled the entire background of the design in pointillé, leaving only the interlacing bands plain.

letter cavity
> The impression made in a matrix or mold used in casting a type of character.

letter hand
> A style of medieval handwriting used in public letters.

letterpress

Any press which gives an impression by bringing together flat surfaces, one of which is called the bed and the other the platen; prints a single sheet by pressing it against an entire frame or chase of type at the same time.

letters, four classes of

The letters of our written alphabet may be divided into four classes relative to a real or imaginary line: linear letters, small letters (miniscules) which are written on the line and go only a short distance above it (a, c, e, i, m, n, o, r, s, u, v, w, and x), no capitals (majuscules) being included in this group; supralinear letters, letters which go a considerable distance above the line (b, d, h, k, l, and t), most of the capital letters belonging to this group; infralinear letters, which go a considerable distance below the line (g, j, p, q, y, and z), only the capitals X and Y being included; double-length letter, which goes a considerable distance above and below the line, our letter f.

Lettre Bâtarde

In addition to the use of pointed and rounded Gothics, medieval German and French printers used various cursive types, especially for works printed in the vernacular. These were known as Bastarda or, in the French, Lettre Bâtarde. They differed from other groups in several respects: the letters f and the long s continued below the base line and were slightly sloped; the short s was closed on the left hand; ascenders were frequently looped, while descenders were often pointed; the letter a was closed and one-storied; the letters m and n, when used to end a word, were usually given a descender tail. The earliest known examples of German Bastarda are found in the famous thirty-line and thirty-one-line Papal Indulgences printed at Mainz in 1454-1455.

Lettre de Forme

A French Textura type: the letters were tall but had short ascenders and descenders which ended in points known as "feet." They were closely compressed and gave the printed page a closely packed appearance. Textura types were cut by the earliest Dutch printers and by Gutenberg and his associates.

Lettre de Somme
  For scholastic and classical texts in Latin, early printers used
  a broader, rounder, less formal letter, known as Fere-Humanistica or, in the French, Lettre de Somme. It was copied from
  more informal book hands and was quite lighter in effect than
  Textura types. The lower part of its letters ended bluntly, but
  it had longer ascenders and descenders. Outstanding example
  of the Fere-Humanistic (Lettre de Somme) type is the Rationale
  Divinorum Officiorum, printed by Fust and Schoeffer in 1459.

Levant morocco
  The finest of all leathers for binding. It is goatskin, called
  morocco from the reputed land of its origin.

lexicography
  Art, process, or occupation of making a lexicon or dictionary.

lexicon
  Originally a synonym for the term bibliography; today, it is
  a wordbook or dictionary, usually of a foreign language, which
  includes definitions of entries and an alphabetical or other
  systematic arrangement.

lexigraphy
  A system of writing in which each character represents a word,
  as that of the Chinese.

liaisons
  Conjoined letters, often found in the Gothic secretary script,
  comparable to what printers call duotypes; that is, two letters
  which are written in such a manner that the terminal stroke of
  the former is the initial stroke of the latter.

libelli
  Wax tablets, discovered in 1875 at Pompeii, which prove that
  by 55-56 A.D. a roman cursive, older than the uncial book
  hand, was in use for letters and business purposes.

Liber Festivalis (1493)
  The first book to bear Wynkyn de Worde's name as a printer
  and to be printed with his own type. Wynkyn de Worde succeeded Caxton to the press when the latter died in 1491.

Liber Studiorum
 The most famous work of J. M. W. Turner, whose major contribution to the art of mezzotint was the application of mezzotint
 work to landscape studies.

library binding
 A binding generally made of strong durable cloth, being a
 compromise between a true binding and a casing. The sewing
 is done by a machine and tapes are glued between split boards.

Library of Congress
 Established in 1800, it is the national library of the United
 States, the repository of books, periodicals, manuscripts,
 and other materials, predominantly American but including
 those of other nations. It receives two copies of every book
 published and copyrighted in the United States and has a lend-
 lease arrangement with libraries throughout the country.

libretto
 The text or words of an opera or any extended choral composi-
 tion--a cantata, for example. It is the diminutive form of the
 Italian libro, book.

libri lintei
 One of the early archives of Rome was the Libri Magistratum,
 or Book of the Magistrates, which records the names and official actions covering a long period of time. Some of these,
 preserved in the Temple of the goddess of memory, Moneta,
 on Capitol Hill, were recorded on linen; whence the name
 libri lintei.

ligature
 The linking of certain letters by means of an unnecessary extra
 stroke. Often the legating stroke is a compound curve or a simple
 right-handed curve extending from the top of the first letter to the
 top of the second one. Careless ligatures are at times mistaken
 for other letters; also, a single character consisting of two or
 more letters or characters which are usually modified in shape
 by being written with a continuous stroke or linked together.

Linear A and Linear B scripts
 Two types of clay tablets and inscribed stones which, since
 the late nineteenth century, have been collected in the vicinity

88

of Knossos on the island of Crete and are associated with the excavations of ruins dating back to 1100 B.C. Linear A remain undeciphered, but Linear B scripts were finally translated in the early 1950's by Michael Ventris, who discovered Linear B script to be an early form of Greek.

linear hieroglyphics
Hieroglyphics of the earliest picture writing which were gradually reduced in later writings to simpler forms, which retained only the leading characteristics of the objects sym- bolized.

line block
An engraving process by which anything in black and white without tones can be reproduced in unlimited quantities. The reproduction may be smaller or larger than the original from which it proceeds. A negative is obtained from the original, from which negative print alone can a line block be made for the print- ing process. The process which employs dots of various sizes and shapes to effect tone through optical illusion is known as halftone block.

line engraving
Made by cutting a line into copper, scraping away the furrow ridge and inking the lines. Popular towards the middle of the sixteenth century, it was used to produce maps, charts, and topographical drawings.

line of spots
A method adopted by the American publishing trade to eliminate signatures. A spot of ink is printed on the outer fold of each sheet or gathering. The spot on the first sheet is near the top of the fold, that on the second is a little lower, that on the third a little lower still, and so on. Thus if a binder takes up a pile of sheets or gatherings, constituting presumably a complete copy of a book, there will be a line of spots extending diagonal- ly across what will be the back of the book.

Linotype
Typesetting and typecasting machines are of two main kinds: those which cast slugs, solid whole lines of type; and those which cast single type characters and then arrange them into lines automatically. The best known machine of the first type

is called the Linotype, patented by Ottmar Mergenthaler in 1885. It carries out simultaneously the operations of assembling, casting, and distribution.

Linotype, operation of
The operator strikes the keys to release matrices from a magazine at the back of the machine. When he has assembled enough for a full line, he pulls a lever that forces the molten metal against the whole line and casts it all in one slug or line of type. Because the letters are not separate, corrections can only be made at the machine by assembling the matrices all over again and casting a new line.

literary forger
The plagiarist tries to get the world to accept as his own what someone else has written. The literary forger tries to make the world accept as the genuine writing of another what he has himself composed.

lithography
A planographic method of illustration, based on the principle that grease attracts grease and water repels it. The design to be printed is drawn with a special lithographic crayon of greasy composition. The stone on which the drawing is made is then "etched" with a mixture of nitric acid, gum arabic, and water. When the stone is inked, the water soaked parts of the surface repel the ink, which is itself a form of grease, and the greasy lines attract it, thus leaving ink only on the lines that are to be printed. The process of lithography was invented by Alois Senefelder in 1798.

Livres D'Heures
(Book of the Hours), one of the most widely published printed books in France around 1500.

locking up of type
The use of wedges or quoins to fit the type so closely together that the whole page or section may be lifted as if all were in one piece.

Lombardic
Belonging to or characteristic of the medieval Italian writing developed from the roman cursive.

**London Polyglot Bible**
The most important polyglot Bible, issued in 1654-1657, edited
by Brian Walton, contains all or part of the Bible in Hebrew,
Samaritan, Aramaic, Syriac, Arabic, Ethiopic, Persian,
Greek (with a literal Latin translation of each), and Latin.
Also known as Walton's Polyglot.

**London Times**
Was started by Walter under the name of Daily Universal Ledger
in 1785.

**Long Roman Primer**
Roman type of ten points, as opposed to Great Primer which
is eighteen points.

**lowercase.** See case.

**lower criticism**
Textual criticism, or criticism which aims to reconstruct the
original texts of the Bible.

**Ludlow, The**
A machine which casts slugs for display work, frequently used
in conjunction with another machine, called the Elrod, which
casts rules, leads, borders, and plain slugs. It does not compose
automatically, as does the Linotype. When all the characters are
in position, the composing being done by hand with the use of a
special stick, the stick is passed into the machine, which casts
the line as a slug, trims it, and ejects it. Succeeding lines are
built by hand as required.

**Lyonnese Bindings**
A sixteenth-century French style, characterized by heavily
tooled strapwork, generally with arabesques on a background
of gold. The impression is done with large dies, but the work,
when well done, is difficult to distinguish from pure hand-
tooled Grolier work. When done poorly, Lyonnese Bindings
are ugly and vulgar, characterized by exaggerated painted or
enamelled strapwork and with all free spaces thickly covered
with semis.

# M

machine-made paper
Paper made in a vibratory trough which causes the fibers of the paper to lie in more or less uniform direction.

machine printed book
Printed by means of stereotype, linotype, electrotype, monotype, or photolithography.

"made perfect"
Said of a book which has been supplied an appropriate leaf from another copy to replace its own missing one. Often, leaves are supplied from wrong editions.

main entries
Listings of books which serve to describe the publication and to differentiate it from all others. They are generally titles or names which define the book as a whole.

Mainz Catholicon
A Latin dictionary written by Joannes Balbus in the 13th century and printed at Mainz in 1460, according to some by Gutenberg. It is a folio of 373 leaves, printed in double columns in a small type, and has a lengthy, although unclear, colophon, which does not reveal the printer.

Mainz Indulgences
Papal documents printed in Mainz in 1454, which prove that the art of printing had attained a high degree of technical excellence by 1454.

Mainz Psalter
Dated 1457, it is the first known publication of Fust and Schoeffer, and the first to contain a definite statement of its date of printing and the names of the printers, the concluding statement of the colophon noting that the work was "diligently brought to completion by Johann Fust, a citizen of Mainz, and Peter Schoeffer of Gernsheim, in the year of the Lord 1457, on the Vigil of the Assumption." It was printed in a new type, larger than any used previously.

Majoli (Maioli) Bindings
　　One of three main Venetian bindings of the late 15th and early
　　16th centuries, named after a Thomasso Maioli (actually Thomas
　　Matthieu), secretary to Catherine de Medici. A famous collector,
　　rather than bookbinder, many of the bindings in his library
　　were decorated with interlacing strapwork combined with medal-
　　lions or sprays of conventional foliage, partly inlaid, partly
　　gold-tooled, achieved either with outline tools or with ajouré
　　or azured tools, that is, tools which had a series of fine paral-
　　lel lines engraved across the design.

majuscules
　　A large letter, capital or uncial, as distinguished from minus-
　　cules, much less commonly used in the fifteenth and sixteenth
　　centuries than today.

Mallermi Bible
　　Published in 1490, it set a new fashion for title-page decoration,
　　the sixteenth century becoming "the age of the woodcut border."
　　The borders of pillars, arches, vines, and scroll work were
　　generally cut in one piece, and the designs, sometimes white
　　with a black ground, were most often formed of black lines
　　upon a white background.

Manière Criblée
　　A method of relief printing, produced from metal plates mounted
　　on wood blocks, with the drawing on the plate being made by means
　　of a graver, so that the lines of the design are sunk beneath the
　　surface and appear as white lines upon a black background when
　　printed. Various shaped punches were used for making dots in the
　　form of stars, diamonds, fleur-de-lis, etc., and additional
　　elaboration of texture was obtained by cross-hatching (a series
　　of crisscross lines with the graver) over the punched parts of
　　the plate. The earliest printed work in this style was produced
　　in 1454, the finest, in the late century, being Livres d'Heures.

marbled paper
　　Paper which has been on a bed of size and has picked up both
　　the color sprinkled there and the design pattern.

margin
　　The blank space around the printed or written area on a page
　　or sheet, differentiated as: head margin, at the top of the page;

tail margin, at the bottom of the page; outer margin, at the
outer edge of the page; inner margin, nearest the fold or back
of the book. The tail margin is the largest margin; the inner
margin is the smallest margin.

marginalia
Notes placed in the margin of a book; marginal notes.

margins, rule of
Traditionally, printers observe the following rule in designing
pages: in such a way that the bottom margin is about twice the
width of the top margin, and the sides of the type areas are
about one-quarter more than the top. The inner margin is partly concealed by the folding and sewing and hence appears to be
the narrowest.

matrix
A metal plate, usually of copper, suitably formed to mold the
face of a type. In a linotype machine, a brass plate having on
its front edge an intaglio of the letter it is to produce in relief.

Maying and Disporte
Produced at Edinburgh by Chepman and Myller; first book
printed in Scotland.

Mazarin Bible
An edition of the Vulgate printed at Mainz about 1450-1455 by
Gutenberg and others, which was the first Bible, and probably
the first completed book, printed with movable metal type; so
called from its being found about 1760 in the Mazarin Library.
Also known as the 42-line Bible and the Gutenberg Bible.

Mearne Binding
Named after the printer Samuel Mearne, it is sometimes called
"Restoration" or 17th-century binding. Its decorations are in
red and black.

measured format
The shape of the publication determined by measuring the height
of the covers.

measure of paper
Includes the following quantities: one quire totals 24 sheets;

one ream totals 20 quires. However, printing press paper is usually sold in reams of 516 sheets (21 1/2 quires). Handmade "art" paper is usually sold in reams of 480 sheets.

mechanical woodpulp
It is produced cheaply and quickly by grinding the wood me-chanically until it is almost sawdust and then pulping it by chemical treatment. Because its fibers are short and full of impurities, and the paper made from it lacks strength and discolors easily, it is used only for newspapers and other works of short-lived interest. Chemical woodpulp is made by first cutting wood into small blocks, usually about an inch square, and then subjecting the blocks to either a soda or a sulphite process, which reduces them to a much purer cellulose with longer and stronger individual fibers. Paper made in this way has greater strength, looks cleaner, and does not change its color so easily; hence it is used a great deal in the produc-tion of everyday books.

merchant's mark
The pictorial symbol used by the merchant or printer.

Merovingian handwriting
Roman cursive hands, after the 7th and 8th centuries A.D., became increasingly modified by national characteristics in the countries where they were used. The resulting forms were: Merovingian in France, Visigothic in Spain, and Beneventam in Italy.

Messkataloge
German trade catalog which marks the beginning of true biblio-graphy.

metal bindings
Finely wrought metal center and corner pieces were used to decorate book covers in medieval times, but the style achieved its greatest popularity during the sixteenth, seventeenth, and eighteenth centuries in England, notably in the small devotional books carried at the girdle by ladies of Henry VIII's court.

metalcut
A means of book illustration by a drawing made on a soft metal block. The use of metal began in the late fifteenth century.

metallography

A substitute for lithography, in which metallic plates, instead of stone, are used.

mezzotint

A form of engraving in intaglio. The surface of a copper or steel plate is first roughened, that is, uniformly pricked with innumerable small holes, usually with a tool called a rocker, which has a curved serrated edge with cutting teeth. The process of roughing not only pricks the plate so that it will hold ink, but it also throws up a burr on the plate surface, which causes the ink to be more deeply absorbed. To obtain lighter tones, the artist removes a little of the burr with a tool called a scraper, so that those portions of the plate will hold slightly less ink.

micro-materials

As library acquisitions began to exceed stack space in the 1930's, new ways of storing large quantities of graphic materials were devised, notably microfilms and, in particular, microcards. Newspapers, periodicals, and government publications were among the first to be reproduced in these forms.

Midwest Interlibrary Center

As book stocks in the larger universities reached unmanageable proportions in the 1930's and 1940's, some universities solved their problem through the use of microfilming and discarding; other universities met the problem through the formation of cooperative interlibrary storage centers, jointly owned and controlled by several universities. The New England Deposit Library in Boston, for example, is maintained by the major libraries of that area, including Harvard and the Massachusetts Institute of Technology. The Midwest Interlibrary Center at Chicago, created in 1951, is owned jointly by some fifteen Middle Western university libraries. In these library depots are deposited newspapers, runs of periodicals, and in general those works for which the demand is occasional or rare.

miniature

Painting in colors, as in medieval manuscripts; an illumination. Any very small painting, especially a portrait, as on ivory or metal; also, the art of painting miniatures.

minims

A single downstroke, as any of the three in the letter m. In the
history of writing, one notes that most of the M's which occur
in Old English manuscripts, up to almost the end of the seventeenth century, are fanciful distortions of the roman M, usually brought about by converting one or more of the straight
strokes (minims and diagonals) into loops, by substituting ties
or bows for angles at the junctions of the diagonals with minims.

minuscules

Any of several styles of ancient and medieval writing developed
from the cursive hand, differing from majuscules in having
simplified and smaller forms, and corresponding to what we
know today as lowercase letters. In medieval times, the main
characteristics of a minuscular script were a reduction in the
size of the letters and an increased tendency for the letters to
pass above or below a base line.

Mirrour of the World

Printed by Caxton in 1481, supposedly one of the earliest books
with illustrations. The other is Parvus et Magnus Cato, also
printed by Caxton.

Misogonus

In the manuscript play of Edmund Ironside, transcribed in the
last decade of the seventeenth century, commas occur very
rarely; colons perform the duty of commas, periods, query
marks, exclamations; only seven question marks occur and
only one exclamation point is used. In the Misogonus, written
in 1577, almost every modern punctuation mark is employed
freely.

monastic bindings

The covers of the finest manuscript editions of the Gospels and
other sacred texts, owned by the richer monastic churches,
were adorned with metals, enamels, and inset jewel work. A
representative cover, still extant, is a copy of the Scriptures
presented by Queen Theodolinda to the Church of Monza in the
6th century, consisting of two plates of gold bearing a cross
set with small cameos and garnets.

monograms

Characters or ciphers, composed of two or more letters inter-

woven or combined, so as to represent a name or part of it.
They occur as ornamental devices in all ages. They are found
on seals, ornamental pins, rings, and buttons; and were frequently used by printers and binders, painters and engravers.

monotype
A machine which casts type characters singly and then arranges
them into lines automatically, invented by Tolbert Lanston of
Ohio in 1887. It has two separate units: a keyboard and a caster.
The more common keyboard contains keys representing 225 type
characters and sorts. The caster unit consists of a metal pot
containing molten type metal, fitted with a mold and with a
chimney for carrying away fumes.

Montaigne Type
A 16-point type designed by Bruce Rogers, one of America's
foremost type and book designers, for a three-volume edition
of the Essays of Montaigne. It was based upon the 15th century-
original of Nicholas Jenson.

Morgan Library
The library is today one of the cultural treasures of the Western
world. When the son opened the library for public reference
use in 1924, it included over 25,000 volumes, in addition to
hundreds of rare manuscripts, cuneiform tablets, drawings,
paintings, prints, medals, and coins--housed in a magnificent
library and preserved with a large endowment.

morocco cloth
In 1825, Archibald Leighton made available to publishers and
binders a cloth of white calico, glazed and dyed at his London
premises. Because it was costly and compared unfavorably with
leather, it was not immediately popular. In the early 1830's,
however, Leighton set up embossing machinery which enabled
him to give this cloth a grained surface resembling that of
morocco. This immediately became popular and several
firms set up machinery to prepare the so-called "morocco
cloth."

morocco leather
Probably the finest leather for binding, durable and flexible;
prepared from goatskin (imitations are made of sheepskin,
etc.), tanned with sumac, or subjected to chrome tanning and
dyed on the grain side. See Levant Morocco.

98

motet
   A polyphonic choral composition on a sacred text, usually without instrumental accompaniment. The oldest, those from about
   1300 have a cantus firmus, for which later composers, for
   example Bach, substitute often the Protestant chorale.

mould (also mold)
   In paper manufacturing, a frame with a wire cloth bottom, on
   which the pulp is drained to form a sheet; more specifically,
   a pattern, hollow form or matrix, which is used for giving
   shape and form to both handmade and machine-made paper,
   in the process of converting the fibers of wood pulp into paper.
   In photoengraving, the grained plate of copper, with the gelatin
   image on it, ready for etching.

movable type
   Generally held to have been invented by Gutenberg. It constituted a significant advance over the use of woodcut letters,
   for it made use of metal-mold letters which could be used
   repeatedly. The invention spread rapidly throughout Europe
   during the thirty years after its inception.

multiple blocks (lithographic)
   A method of color illustration whereby the black part of the
   picture is first cut alone on one block and printed as the "key";
   after which another block is printed for, say, the color red,
   and so on.

Muratorian Fragment
   Contains the earliest known list of books of the New Testament.

# N

Narmer Tablet
In it is evidenced the possible transition from pictographic to ideographic and phonetic writing. The picture of an eye was a pictograph for eye and an ideograph for see; and the meaning eye could be made plain by prefixing the phonogram for m' (eye) as a determinative.

narrow entry words
They are extremely precise and lead the user to very definite subjects or topics of discussion.

Nash Papyrus
The oldest known biblical fragment; contains in Hebrew the text of the Ten Commandments and dates back to the first century after Christ.

national bibliography
Lists of books published in a given country; also books or works by natives of the given country which are published abroad.

national handwriting
Roman cursive handwriting modified by national characteristics. Examples are Merovingian, Visigothic, and Beneventan.

Negligent Capitals
A script (also designated Rustic) characterized by letters which are angular, square, irregular, and formed of broken strokes with circumflex finals. It continued in fashion till the sixth or seventh century, but was not abandoned till the ninth. One of the oldest books in existence in which this script is used (in a Latin alphabet) is the famous Codex Romanus, a copy of Virgil's Aeneid, preserved in the Vatican. It is believed to date back to the third century A.D.

Neo-Caroline hand (Carolingian Minuscule)
Used by scribes in the fifteenth century as they copied works from classic and pre-Christian literature. The use of the Neo-Caroline hand accentuated the interest in fine calligraphy

and seemed a blessing to those scholars and collectors who looked upon the "Gothic" style as barbarous.

Newberry Library
One of the major research libraries in Chicago. Founded in 1887 by Walter L. Newberry as a public reference library in the humanities and social sciences, it also possesses an exceptional collection of books on typography.

News, The
The first Russian newspaper. Founded by Peter the Great in 1703, with himself as editor; he filled his position by clipping items from foreign newspapers.

New York Public Library
Organized in January 1849, with Washington Irving as its first president. The largest public library in the United States, it has many noteworthy special collections, including 140 volumes of eighteenth-century MSS. and 150 volumes of medieval MSS. from the tenth to the sixteenth centuries, largely liturgical and biblical.

nick
The notch on the body of type, which serves two purposes: it enables the compositor to easily determine the correct position of the type, since the nick is always in the belly of the type; it enables the compositor to quickly differentiate kinds of type, since one may have a narrow furrow or nick, while another may have a wide furrow or nick.

Niger
A soft skin with a rather smooth variable grain; a kind of Morocco (goatskin). It is a skin very difficult to imitate.

Nitrian Syriac Manuscript, The
A showpiece of the British Museum Library, and an extremely eminent collection for the understanding of the early Christian Church. This version of the Bible in the Syriac language was discovered by Robert Curzon in the Nitrian Desert of Western Egypt in 1836. It was ultimately acquired from the monks in the Syrian monastery by Henry Tatum. The entire collection contains 317 volumes, mostly written at Edessa or Tekrit, the latest bearing the date 1292, the earliest bearing the date 411.

# O

Octavo
> A work of sheets each of which is folded into eight leaves; hence, a more or less definite size of book so made. A folio is a work made of sheets folded once (two leaves, four pages to the sheet); a quarto is a work made of sheets folded twice to form four leaves and eight pages; an octavo is a work made of sheets folded three times to form eight leaves and sixteen pages. The size of octavos (of any format) differs according to the size of paper which is used for printing, hence: cap octavo, 4 1/4 x 11 1/2 inches; crown octavo, about 5 x 7 1/2 inches; demy octavo, 5 1/2 x 8 inches; imperial octavo, 8 1/4 x 11 1/2 inches; medium octavo, 6 x 9 1/2 inches (the size commonly meant by octavo unqualified); post octavo, 5 1/2 x 7 1/2 inches; royal octavo, 6 1/2 x 10 inches. According to the American Library Association scale, an octavo is more than 20 cm. and not over 25 cm. in height.

oddments
> In the mind of the printer, the book properly begins with the introduction or first chapter and ends with the last page of the final chapter. Anything which is outside of these limits is considered oddments.

offset lithography
> A printing process in which an inked impression (usually from a dampened planographic surface) is first made on a rubber-blanketed cylinder and then transferred to the paper being printed.

Old Face Type
> A refinement, in a sense, of the Jenson type, first used by Aldus Manutius of Venice. The earliest Old Face type was first used in an edition of Cardinal Bembo's De Aetna, printed in 1495, and was especially popular in the 16th century. It is distinguished by its graceful irregularity, its slanted ascender serifs, and by the slight contrast between light and heavy strokes.

**opening**
> Two pages in a book which face each other.

**open sheet**
> Format used for printing maps, proclamations, and the like; spoken of as open sheet folio or broadside.

**opistograph**
> A manuscript, slab, or the like, written or inscribed on both the back and the front.

**Oratio**
> When this work of Wakefield was printed in England by De Worde in 1524, it marked the introduction of italics and the first English attempt to cut Arabic and Hebrew letters.

**Oriental palm leaf book**
> A book made by tying sheets of palm leaf together by means of holes at two ends. The writing was scratched in and rubbed over with lamp black.

**orihon**
> The earliest papyrus books comprised long rolls across which the text was written on one side of the material only. Later the text was written along the roll, but divided into columns for easy reading. A third method resulted from flattening the roll and then folding it concertina-wise down the spaces between the columns of text, forming individual pages, each of which contained one column of written matter. The blank backs of these pages were pasted together and holes were pierced down the left-hand side of the entire book, which was then bound by strips of leather or cord which were passed through the holes. A papyrus book thus folded and bound was known as an orihon.

**ornamental initials**
> Large capital letters, woodcuts or metal castings, which were used at the beginning of a chapter or paragraph. They often provide the only identification of the printer of the book.

**orthography**
> The art or system of spelling.

overcasting
   A process in binding in which the folds of paper are sewn together beyond the ordinary sewing; generally used for the first
   and last sections of books.

Oxford Lectern Bible
   Printed in 1935, it is generally regarded as an outstanding piece
   of modern book production. It also illustrates an impressive
   use of the Centaur type, which was produced commercially
   by the Monotype Corporation in 1929.

Oxford, printing at
   The first book printed at Oxford was the Expositio Sancti
   Ieronimi in Simbolum Apostolorum, a treatise on the Apostles'
   Creed by Rufinus, Bishop of Aquileia. The printing date is 1478.

Oxford University Library. See Bodleian Library.


# P


page
   A single side of a leaf in a book or newspaper.

page, righthand of
   All parts of a book, other than the chapters, are placed or begin
   on a right-hand page; for example, bastard title, title page, dedication, preface, list of contents, list of illustrations.

pagination
   The act or process of paging a book; that is, assigning numbers
   or characters to the individual pages.

paging
   Whether the type is set by hand or by machine, it cannot be

printed as a book while it lies in slabs on galleys. The slabs
must first be divided into page lengths with all their accessories--
headings, footnotes, etc.

paging, responsibility for
Paging is done by the clicker or, under his supervision, by
compositors. The clicker is the foreman of the composing
room, who receives the work to be done and apportions it
among the members of his group, watches its progress, and
advises on any difficulties that may arise.

painted bindings
Books bound in wooden boards with pictures painted upon them.
Especially popular in Italy in the 14th and early 15th centuries.

paleography
The study of ancient modes of writing including inscriptions;
the art or science of deciphering ancient writings, determining
their origin, period, etc.

paleology
The study or knowledge of antiquities, especially prehistoric
antiquities.

palimpsest
A parchment, tablet, or other portion of writing material,
which has been used twice or three times (double palimpsest),
the earlier writing having been erased; a manuscript in which
one or two earlier erased writings are found; a codex rescriptus.

pallet
A tool, like a part of a fillet, used chiefly in gilding the backs
of books. It can be used to letter a whole word, name, or title
in one operation, as opposed to building it up by the impression of a series of single-letter tools.

panel
Any area on a book cover enclosed by a tooled or stamped
border and having a polished or natural surface; a label affixed or inserted, on which tooling, stamping, or finishing
may be done. A parallel binding is one, for example, with a
rectangle, formed of single, double, or triple fillets, gilt
or blind, either on the sides or between the bands on the spine
of the book.

panel stamps

They were cut on latten, a metal alloy similar to brass, the thin engraved plate being fixed by pegs to a wooden block. The impression was made on the leather through the use of a hammer or weights or, later, through the use of a binder's press. At first English panel stamps contained only binder's initials, not his full name. In time, however, the heraldic motif became prominent in English panel stamps.

paper

Material composed of vegetable fibers intertwined with each other so as to form a sheet upon which it is possible to write. First the raw material (rags, esparto, bark, wood) is reduced to a thin pulp. The pulp is then run upon a flat sieve of fine mesh, which retains the fibers that become felted together. Then follow the processes of drying, bleaching, sizing, pressing, tinting, etc.

paper, varieties of

art paper  Paper with a special coating of glazed china clay, making it the smoothest possible surface on which to print halftone blocks of fine screen. It is, however, very heavy and brittle and often breaks free from books.

cartridge paper  A strong, tough paper, originally used in the manufacture of cartridges. The surface is similar to that of good antique, although harder.

engine-sized  Paper in which the size is mixed with the pulp to become an integral part of the paper.

imitation art  The coating in real art paper is applied after the paper is made, forming a layer on the surface; in imitation art paper, the clay is mixed in with the pulp, a less expensive process, but resulting in a paper inferior to real art.

India  First made for the Oxford University Press, known best for its extraordinary thinness, weight, and opacity. It is especially useful for works which contain many pages and would be too bulky if printed on ordinary paper.

loaded  Not a distinct type of paper; all papers are to a degree loaded in some way; that is, mixed, in the pulp stage, with substances such as kaolin or french chalk or titanium, designed to make the paper smoother or more opaque.

machine-finished  Moderately smooth and shiny, but not glossy. It prints well and allows for a wide range of grades. At its best it is pleasant and useful; at its worst, it is quite undesirable.

marbled  Veined, spotted, or mottled with irregular markings or with a blending of spots and streaks. Especially desirable as endpapers, marbled paper was used much more commonly in former times.

mold-made  Characterized by feathery deckles of handmade papers. Although not so strong as handmade, mold-paper is quite desirable. It is less expensive than handmade paper and is particularly suitable for limited editions as a substitute for handmade paper.

offset  Has a smooth surface, is free from fluff, and is treated with a special sizing. It is a generally pleasant paper, used at times in ordinary letterpress books.

patterned  Papers patterned in relief with some design or other are often used for jackets or bindings. A popular design or pattern is one which simulates leather, achieved by passing the paper as it comes from the machine through rollers engraved with the pattern.

supercalendered  Papers which receive smooth finish by repeated rolling between hot and cold rollers. They provide good results from type and passable results from halftones, and are sometimes used for books in which fine-line blocks or halftones are included in the text.

tub-sized  Sized, like hand-papers, after they are made. They are harder and tougher than engine-sized paper.

woven or laid  Wove paper, held to the light, shows an even, characterless, structure; laid paper shows a series of closely spaced parallel lines with bolder and more widely spaced lines running at right angles. Laid papers are more commonly used in writing and wrapping papers. All papers are generally either laid or wove.

papyri, Egyptain (principal ones extant)
   Abbott Papyrus   A law text, in British Museum.

   Amherst Papyri   Law texts, in possession of Lord Amherst.

   Anastasi Papyri   Narratives, in the British Museum.

   Berlin Papyri   Tales, in the Berlin Museum.

   Ebers Papyrus   A medical text.

   Harris Papyrus   Varied contents; the longest known (135 feet), in British Museum.

   D'Orbiney Papyrus   The "Tale of the Two Brothers," in British Museum.

   Prisse Papyrus   A moral text, in the Bibliotheque Nationale.

   Rhind Papyrus   Mathematics; in the British Museum.

   Sallier Papyri   Of varied contents; in British Museum.

   Turin Papyri   Partly chronological.

papyri, kinds of
   Pliny the Elder differentiates nine varieties: (1) Regia, the
   largest sheet; (2) Livia, the same size as Regia, but thinner;
   (3) Hieratica, a large paper of fine quality, distinguished
   for its whiteness and preferred by the priest for the symbolism
   of white; (4) Amphitheatrica, named for the factory near the
   amphitheater in Alexandria; (5) Fanniana, manufactured at
   Rome; (6) Saitica, an inferior type made at Sais in Egypt;
   (7) Taeniotica, a common variety which was made at Alexandria and was sold by weight instead of by sheet; (8) Em-
   poretica, wrapping paper; (9) Charta Claudia, a strong paper
   in large sheets capable of bearing writing on both sides and
   fabricated by command of the Emperor Claudius. Papyrus
   was the material of virtually all the books of antiquity, until
   it was replaced by vellum.

papyrology
   Study of papyri or papyri manuscripts.

papyrus

Writing material, made from the stalks of the papyrus, a tall
flowering plant which grew along the banks of the Nile. Its
stalks were cut into two-foot lengths and split downwards into
wafer-thin strips with a needle or sharp knife. Several of these
strips were then laid side by side on a board and coated with
a paste made from a mixture of flour and Nile mud. Across
these, other strips were laid at right angles. Thus assembled,
the sheet was either hammered or put into a press, dried in
the sun, and polished with a bone tool so that its surface could
be written on with a soft quill. Papyrus was introduced as a
writing material by the Egyptians in about 3400 B.C., and was
used regularly until the introduction of parchment.

Paradise Lost

The 1902 edition is considered to be the finest work of the Doves
Press and the most beautiful edition of the poem ever printed.

paragraph indention

Should be consistent through a work. It is usually found to equal
one em of the type size in use.

parchment

A writing material which is prepared from the inner side of the
split skin of a sheep. Legend holds that it was invented in the
2nd century B.C. by Eumenes, King of Pergamun, an ancient
city of Mysia (whence its other name Charta Pergamena). It
was probably used as early as 1500 B.C. and is still used for
formal and decorative documents, such as diplomas.

Paris Polyglot Bible

Issued in 1628 and again in 1645 at Paris by Antoine Vitre; of
slight critical value.

partial entries

Sometimes called added entries, they refer to only a part of
the principal entry.

pasteboards

Wooden boards were used for bindings until about the end of
the fifteenth century, when the idea of pasting several layers
of paper together was thought of. The use of pasteboards
for binding roughly coincides with the introduction of printing.

paste-up, procedure of
First a blank dummy of the correct number of pages and the correct size is made, with the pages grouped as they will finally have to be printed. Pictures, if any, are then cut out and pasted into the dummy in the positions in which they shall appear when finally printed; block proofs are pasted down in such a way as to provide the exact margins desired; all provisions are made for legends and illustrations.

peel
A signboard-like object used to pick up the folded sheets from the printing press to hang on lines strung across the room to dry the ink.

pegs on panel stamps
Pegs were used to fix engraved plates on wooden blocks, and impressions were made on the leather either by the use of a hammer or by means of weights on both hammer and weights. In time some of the pegs became loose, and panel stamps are frequently found in which the impression from the loosened pegs can be seen.

Pelasgic Script
The script of the earliest settlers of Greece; important to us because from it derived, by successive modifications, all the subsequent Latin (Italian) alphabets.

perfecting
The printing of the other side of a sheet already printed on one side.

perfecting press
A press that prints the paper on both sides in one passage; sometimes, one that also folds and pastes it.

Perpetua Type
The most successful book type designed by Eric Gill (1882-1940) for the Monotype Corporation in 1929.

Persian Binding
Persian manuscripts of the seventeenth to the nineteenth centuries, bound in pasteboards like other Oriental bindings, were often ornamented in an interesting way. A thin layer of a

kind of gesso was applied on the covers and then painted over,
sometimes with historical and hunting scenes, more often, with
flowers. When finished, the painting was thickly varnished over.

petroglyph
A carving or inscription upon a rock, especially a prehistoric
one.

petrography
Description and systematic classifications of rocks.

philology
The study of the cultures of civilized peoples as revealed chiefly
in their languages and literatures and religions; also, the study
of language as such--grammar, etymology, phonology, morphology,
semantics, textual criticism, mythology, folklore, etc.

phonogram
A character or symbol used to represent a word, syllable, or
single speech sound. In the history of writing, the phonogram
is preceded by ideogram and, before it, pictogram. In Chinese
writing, a compound character consisting of a radical and a
phonetic.

photographic composing machines
These may eventually replace type completely. By means of a
photographic composing machine, an image is obtained which
can be used to make plates for printing by lithography.

photogravure
Any of several processes for making prints from an intaglio
plate prepared by photographic methods; also, a print made by
this process. Invented in 1879 by Karl Klic of Annau, the technique is employed chiefly to reproduce oil paintings, photographs,
and other forms of illustration.

photogravure, process of
The original picture is photographed upon negative material,
from which a positive transparency is made. Then a close screen
of fine lines crossing each other at right angles is placed over a
carbon tissue (a paper base coated with gelatine and made sensitive to light by treatment with potassium bichromate). The process
ultimately depends on the effect of light in rendering bichromated

111

gelatin or bitumen insoluble, an image being thus obtained from
which the plate can be prepared by etching, molding, or electrotyping.

photo-lithography

A process by which a lithographic picture or copy from a
design is produced photographically, with the image forming
the design being produced on the stone directly or by transfer.
Invented by Senefelder. Instead of his limestones, however,
which are heavy and awkward to handle, thin zinc or aluminum
plates are now used.

photo-lithography, process

The plate is first put into a special machine which roughens its
surface so that water will adhere to it. It is then photo-sensi-
tized with a coating of albumen and ammonium bichromate.
The design to be reproduced is photographed in the usual way.
The negative is then placed over the sensitized plate and held
in position by vacuum, and the plate is exposed to strong light
until the whole thickness of the film under the clear portions
of the negative is rendered insoluble. Thus prepared, the plate
is inked with a thin, greasy lithographic ink and then washed
with water, which dissolves the inky emulsion not hardened by
the action of the light. Finally, the plate is rinsed, given an
"etch," re-rinsed, dried, and given a thin even coating of gum
arabic solution. It is allowed to stand for a time before being
used for printing.

photo-litho offset

Discovered in 1903-1904 by an American lithographer named
Ira W. Rubel. In this process, the positive design upon the
original plate is printed upon a rubber blanket, upon which it
appears in reverse, and from which it is then offset, appearing
as a positive on the paper. The term offset itself is used in the
printing trade to signify a more or less distinct transfer of type
impression to the back of the next sheet delivered from the
press, when the sheets are laid together before the ink is dry.

photo-litho offset process

The offset press consists of three cylinders: a revolving plate
cylinder which prints the design; a rubber blanket cylinder
which receives the design from the plate cylinder; and an impression cylinder which carries the paper upon which the

design is transferred from the blanket cylinder. Modern rotary presses are capable of printing up to 7,000 impressions or more per hour.

pi
Any disordered heap of type. Earlier, when all type was founders' type, pi was given to an apprentice to sort out and distribute back into the case; today, with monotype, it is simply shot into a box to be melted down for the caster.

pica
Pica was once the unity by which furniture, length of line of type, depth of page, and other things were measured. Today pi is the size of type, 12 points in depth, commonly used by printers as the standard of measurement for width of lines, etc. With no qualification, the word em in virtually every printing house designates twelve-point em and en. The twelve-point em is almost a sixth of an inch, since seventy-two points are just a shade under an inch.

pictogram
The earliest form of writing consisting of pictures of objects. The ideogram and phonogram follow pictogram in development. Also written pictograph.

pictorial initial letter
The first letter of a word which is made to stand out by the decorative quality of the letter. Most often used at the beginning of chapters or of paragraphs.

picture prints
The art of cutting a design in relief upon a block of wood, which was then inked and printed from, was used by the Chinese to print fabrics as early as the 9th century A.D. But the art of printing upon paper was introduced into Europe at the beginning of the 15th century. The earliest prints were of simple religious pictures in outline, produced in the monasteries.

picture prints with words
From picture prints it was a simple step to the production of leaflets which contained both pictures and words. At first only single words were introduced, but as the woodcutters became more skilled, whole sentences were incorporated. The leaf-

lets were called <u>Einblattdrucke</u>, distributed by priests and wandering monks to their congregations as illustrations of their sermons.

picture writing
The earliest certain monuments of the Babylonians and Sumerians support the traditional theory of pictographic origin.

pigskin
Perhaps the most familiar of all bookbinding leathers. It is a thick, rich leather, suitable for large books, not small ones. Treated with lime, it was the favored material for the covering of fine German books of the fifteenth, sixteenth, and seventeenth centuries.

<u>Pinakes</u>
Either a catalogue of the Alexandrian Library, or a union catalogue of the principal libraries of the metropolis. In this famous, but unfortunately, lost work, Callimachus distinguished five classifications of subject matter: (1) Poetry, (2) History, (3) Philosophy, (4) Oratory, and (5) Miscellaneous.

pinhead grain
About the middle of the nineteenth century it was discovered that, if the process of straight graining was carried out a second time at right angles to the first operation, the little furrows and ridges were broken up and a surface was produced with minute pinheads.

piracy, literary
Any unauthorized appropriation and reproduction of another's production, invention, or idea; literary or artistic theft. For a violation of copyright, the term <u>infringement</u> is more precise.

pirated edition
A work produced and marketed without the authority of, or payment to, the author.

plank
That part of the printing press on which was fastened the forme of type. It had iron shoes on the under side which slid on iron nails.

planography
A process of printing from a flat or plane surface, as from stone, zinc, aluminum, in lithographic processes or offset printing.

planten
At the bottom of the hand printing press, a piece of mahogany four-inches thick, on the top of which is fixed a small steel center hole in which the toe of the screw works. In offset printing, the platen is a rotating cylinder.

plaster-process
A system used mainly between the years 1802-1846, whereby molds were formed in papier mâché before being cast in metal.

plate
A polished sheet of copper or steel (or aluminum) which is used to print from.

plate line
When the paper is larger than the plate, there will be a margin between the part that has been pressed and smoothed and the outside margin. The line that encloses the pressed portion is called the plate line.

platen press
The simplest form of power-driven press. It employs the same basic principles as the hand press, the printing being accomplished by the action of a flat surface known as the platen in pressure upon the type carried upon another flat surface known as the bed. Most power-operated platen presses are similar in design.

playing cards
First made in the fourteenth century, playing cards represent an important step in the development of the art of illustration. Playing cards were printed from woodcut blocks and were hand colored by means of stencils. German woodcutters produced playing cards in great quantities.

pointillé
Based upon the complicated fanfare binding with its interlacing strapwork, but with scrolls and other ornaments in dotted lines instead of unbroken ones. First used about the year 1640. The

style is associated vaguely with Le Gascon, who is said to have brought the design to its highest development and to have become the finest of binders.

points
Something similar to drawing-pins; they were attached to the tympan sheet so that, when the tympan was folded down, the points would fall on the line equally distant from the top of the pages and pierce holes in the sheet of paper. When the sheets came to be perfected (printed on the other side), the pin holes fitted the pins and a perfect register was made.

point system
A system according to which the various sizes of type bodies, leads, etc., bear a fixed and simple relation to one another. The point system now in general use in America was adopted in 1886 by the United States Type Founders' Association, though many founders were already using it. It is a modification of a French system, and is based upon the pica body then most used. This body is divided into twelfths, called "points," and every type body consists of a given number of these points. The value of the point is .013837 inch, or nearly 1/72 inch.

Pompeian Diptychs
A large collection of small wax writing tablets or Pugilaria found during some excavations at Pompeii in 1875. They are of wood and resemble small slates, one side being slightly hollowed out to receive a filling of blackened wax. Two, and sometimes three and even more, of the tablets were hinged together, like a tail or "Caudex," from which the word Codex is said to derive. They are the direct prototypes of modern books.

porcelain types
The Chinese are known to have had types of clay or porcelain in the eleventh century. They set them up in a frame, printed from them, and later cut the original types in wood, from which they made impressions or stereotypes in porcelain. After baking the porcelain, they cast leaden types from it.

Portiforia
Small breviaries intended to be carried about.

portraits in watermarks
 In 1904 there was a German exhibit at the St. Louis Exhibition,
 which showed the remarkable effect achieved by impressing
 paper pulp by means of a photographic plate in relief. Set up
 in a frame with a light behind them, they looked like very
 delicate paintings in monotone. Most were portraits of cele-
 brities.

post of sheets
 A stack of alternate paper and felt.

pot
 A term sometimes used to designate the smallest size paper.

pot cassé
 A device used by one of the most influential printers, born at
 Bourges in about 1480. It consisted of a broken jar pierced by
 a wimble (for which the French word was tonet), and usually
 accompanied by the motto Non Plus. Several of his engravings
 bore the device of the Lorraine cross.

practical bibliography
 Research, compilation of notes and bibliography, preparation
 of manuscript for press, etc.

Praenestine Fibula
 The earliest extant monument of Latin writing is the inscription
 dating from about 600 B.C., in the so-called archaic alphabet,
 and written from right to left. The Duenos (vase) inscription
 and the Black Stone of the Forum are other famous examples
 of this archaic alphabet. (Fibula is the lower part of the human
 leg from the knee to the ankle.)

Prayer Book Type
 A special printing type, published in 1903; specially designed
 for use in the Prayer Book of King Edward VII.

prayer wheels
 Prayers written on strips which are rolled up inside Buddhist
 prayer wheels. Instead of reading the prayer, however, the
 wheels are simply rolled, the revolution being equivalent to the
 prayer being read. Each line of manuscript runs along the

entire length of the roll, which is unrolled sideways. Variously ornamented, the best known are the relatively small ones chiefly used in Thibet.

Preface

A short introductory statement printed at the beginning of a book or article (or separate from it) in which the author states his purpose in writing, makes necessary acknowledgments of assistance, comments on the difficulties and uncertainties encountered in the writing of the work and, in general, informs the reader of those facts which he thinks pertinent to the reading of the text.

preliminaries

All those pages which precede the commencement of the text proper; that is, half or bastard title, title page, preface, list of contents, list of illustrations, etc.

presentation copy

Generally, a book that is the gift of the author; a book, that is, which is spontaneously given by the author. A book which is signed in response to an owner's request, is properly termed an inscribed copy.

Press Licensing Act of 1662

This effected the reduction of the number of London printers to twenty.

press number

A small figure appearing between 1680-1823 at the foot of the page, sometimes twice in a gathering (once on the outer forme, once on the inner forme). It appears to have served as a record of the work done on a particular printing press and as a check on the pressman's claims for pay.

press-rolls

Served to squeeze out water from the pulp and to smooth the surface of the paper.

Prigilaria

Wood tablet notebooks used in early times to record memoranda. See Diptychs.

**primary binding**
Distinguished from secondary or remainder bindings; that is, the first or earliest of several publisher's binding styles found on copies of the same edition.

**primer type**
A size of type: long primer (10 point); great primer (18 point).

**Prime staves**
In ancient times, almanacs were cut on flat pieces of metal, bone, horn, box, fir, or oak in Denmark and Sweden. They are generally hinged along one side by cords run through holes, several slabs in this way being fastened together. These are also known as Rune staves or stocks, Messe dag staves, or Brim stocks. Wooden calendars have also been found among primitive peoples in Sumatra and other places.

**princeps**
First, original; used especially of a first edition or copy belonging to the first edition.

**printer's device**
A monogram or other device used by a printer as a trademark.

**printer's devil**
A young apprentice in a printing office who does chores, and often becomes very black with dust or ink (whence the name).

**printer's ink**
A very viscous substance made from linseed oil and lampblack, a fine soot.

**printer's reader**
The individual whose task it is to discover any errors that may have been made in the setting up of type, and to indicate instructions for their corrections. He also watches for all other possible errors, for example those made even by the author of the text.

**printing**
The art or practice of impressing letters, characters, or figures on paper, including typesetting and presswork; typography.

printing, important dates in
>770, Japanese block-prints; 1041-1049, Japanese movable types;
1392, metal type cast in Korea; 1454, printing in Holland, Mainz;
1460, printing in Germany, Bamberg, and Strassburg; 1465,
printing in Italy, Subiaco; 1470, printing in Paris, France;
1468, printing in Basel, Switzerland; 1474, printing in Valentia,
Spain; 1482, printing in Denmark; 1489, printing in Portugal;
1495, printing in Sweden; 1477, printing in Westminster, England (William Caxton).

printing in the seventeenth century
>This period is generally recognized to have been the worst in
England and Europe.

printing, introduction into American Colonies
>Some printing presses are known to have been brought to Mexico
and elsewhere by the Spaniards. Nonetheless, the real beginning
of printing in America dates from 1639 when, according to Governor Winthrop's Diary, a printing house was opened by Stephen
Daye. The first item printed was the freeman's oath, following
this an almanac, and then the famous Bay Psalm Book (1640),
the earliest surviving American book.

printing, introduction into England
>Printing came to England in 1476, when William Caxton set up
his famous press at Westminster. The first works printed in
England were probably pamphlets. The first dated book printed
in England (in English) was Caxton's Dictes or Sayings of the
Philosophers (1477).

private press
>Originally, it was a press operated solely for the personal
satisfaction of its owner, whose books were not sold for profit.
It has been very successful in England. Among the famous
English private presses should be noted: The Strawberry Hill
Press, 1757; The Daniel Press, 1863; The Kelmscott Press,
1891; The Ashendene Press, 1894; The Vale Press, 1896; The
Doves Press, 1900.

Procurator Bibliothecarum
>An administrative position in a Roman library. It was generally
awarded to a recognized scholar, to whom the bibliothecarus
(librarian) was responsible.

prolegomenon
A preliminary discourse, remark, or observation; a preface,
as to a treatise. Generally used in the plural.

proof
A trial impression, as from type, taken for correction or
examination.

Protat Block
A fragment of wood which is clearly a stamp and can be stylis-
tically dated about 1370. It was discovered in 1902 in a partition
wall of an old house near Dijon, France. It is apparently the
earliest extant example of its kind on which there is a definite
agreement.

protocolum
The first leaf of a codex.

Proto-Semitic
Regarded by some paleographers as the missing link in the
chain of Phoenician writing. These inscriptions, recently
discovered on the Sinaitic peninsula, are dated, on the evidence of pottery found with them, at about 1500 B.C. There is
an obvious resemblance between them and Egyptian writing.

provenance
The origin, source, or provenience of scrolls, manuscripts,
incunabula, etc.

provincialism in bibliography
Few if any scholars are equally familiar with all languages.
This is especially true in America as regards to Slavic and
oriental languages. There are also limitations of time and
space. In addition, the bibliographer has difficulty laying his
hands on a publication of which he has heard a great deal.

Psalter
The first book with a printed date and printing in two colors
(1457). See Bible.

publisher's casing
The method of binding books in uniform style by mass production methods and in relatively large quantities, as contrasted
with hand binding and literary binding.

publisher's cloth bindings
The earliest use of cloth for edition binding by publishers came at the beginning of the 1820's, when unsized dress materials such as silk and satin were used to cover "elegant" editions.

publisher's copyright
During the manuscript period of the Middle Ages, neither author nor publisher copyright existed. Outside the monastery, there were no means by which an author could control the duplication of his work, once he parted with his original manuscript or a copy of it. In time, the publisher took steps to ensure that his work would not be published by rival concerns to the detriment of his own sales. But it was not until 1709 that authors had any legal safeguards.

pugillaria
In Rome, during the first seven centuries A.D., small wooded tablets were used for recording memoranda. They were slightly hollowed on one side, the hollow being filled with wax upon which writing could be scratched with a stylus. Sometimes two or three of them were hinged together, thus forming a tablet book. Notebooks of this sort were known as pugillaria.

pulled type
Individual types jerked from the forme by ink-balls.

pulp
The mixture of rag or wood fibers, of which paper is made, when ground up and suspended in water or treated chemically.

pulpitum
In the twelfth and thirteenth centuries, manuscript codices were kept in book chests; but by the end of the thirteenth and early fourteenth centuries they were out of the armaria and on desk bookcases, called pulpitum.

punch
In typefounding, a steel die with a letter formed in relief on its face, so as to enable it to form in copper an intaglio impression that serves as a matrix for casting type. The stamping is done with force.

punch engraving

Punch engraving had been used by goldsmiths and ornament
engravers long before it was used as a method of illustration.
The tools--a small pointed punch, set in a wooden handle and
worked by hand pressure, and larger punches with plain or
grained striking surfaces intended for use with a hammer--
were used to engrave the plate.

punctuation marks in early fonts

| | |
|---|---|
| / | is used for the comma, or to indicate a pause in reading; |
| ? | seems to have been used in England from about 1521; |
| : | is found in books printed in England about 1580-1590, but no origin is known; |
| ; | seems to have been first used in England about 1569, but not common until 1580; |
| . | was commonly used before as well as after the roman and arabic numerals until about 1580; |
| ' | was used in contractions (i.e., t's instead of 'tis) in Elizabethan times; |
| " | were used, until late in the 17th century, at the beginning of the line to call attention to sententious remarks. Such passages are not quotations; |
| ( ) | often used in the 16th century where today we use quotation marks; |
| [ ] | were used in Elizabethan times where today we use parentheses. |

Purifica della Conscientia

In this work of 1512, probably by St. Thomas Aquinas, is
found the first fully engraved title page. It was published at
Florence.

# Q

quad
> (From quadrat.) A block of type metal lower than the letters, and one-half, one, two, or three ems in width, used in spacing and in blank lines.

quad crown
> A sheet of paper measuring thirty by forty inches.

quad demy
> A sheet of paper measuring thirty-five and one-half by forty-five inches.

quadding-out
> The centering of the lines of print upon the page in keeping with the given line.

quad large
> A card measuring six by nine inches.

quad royal
> A sheet of paper measuring forty by fifty inches.

quad small
> A card measuring five by seven inches.

quadrat. See quad.

Quadrata (or Square Capital) hand
> The style of manuscript writing which prevailed during the first Roman period from the 2nd to the 8th century A.D. Its characteristic is a rigid, square, capital letter obviously based upon the formal inscriptional lettering of the time, cut with a chisel in stone.

quarter binding
> Only the spine is leather covered.

quarto

A book of the size of one-fourth of the unfolded sheet of printing paper. To produce a quarto, each sheet of paper, before it is sewn, is folded twice, making four leaves and eight pages of the finished books. On one side of the sheet will be printed pages 1, 4, 5, and 8; on the other side will be printed pages 2, 3, 6, and 7. The type pages that produce 1, 4, 5, and 8 are termed the outer forms (they are on the outside of the sheet after the folding); those that produce 2, 3, 6, and 7 are called inner forms. The expression "in fours" hence signifies a gathering which consists of four leaves; the expression "in eights" signifies a gathering which consists of eight leaves. In a quarto, the chain lines are horizontal, and the watermark is in the middle of the back of pages four and five.

quaternion

Four sheets of vellum fitted into each other, so that when pressed together they made a solid gathering. Loosely, a sheet of paper folded twice.

queen note

Paper measuring three and one-half by five and three-eights inches.

query mark. See punctuation marks.

quinternions

In medieval libraries or monasteries, vellum leaves cut to the required size and fitted inside each other in groups of five. The leaves were marked lightly and sent to the scribe to be written upon.

quipus

Colored pieces of string knotted in a certain way and used by the Incas as a method of record keeping.

quire

A set of twenty-four or twenty-five sheets of paper of the same size and stock. Also, vellum sheets given a single fold down the middle and fitted inside of each other. They were bound together and placed between wooden boards to prevent curling.

quoins
> Wedge-shaped wooden or metal blocks which are used to lock up type in a galley or forme.

quotation mark
> It seems to have been adopted with greater reluctance by pen-man than any other punctuation mark.

# R

rag paper
> A paper material, generally made from a combination of linen and cotton; produces the most durable paper.

raised bands
> When a book is bound, the gathered sections are sewn on to horizontal cords or bands, four or five in number. When the boards are covered, the cords or bands are usually sunk in grooves to make a flat spine; if they are not, they stand out in the form of ridges and are known as <u>raised</u> <u>bands</u>.

ramie
> A high quality paper which is normally used for textiles and bank notes.

ream
> Originally a quantity of paper, usually twenty quires, or 480 sheets. Later, an attempt was made to round out the figure to 500 sheets, but the number has not become a standard. The printer's perfect ream is 516 sheets, because it allows for spoilage in printing and binding and permits calculation on a basis of 500's and over. All three reams are used at present.

rectangular style bindings
   A form of bookbinding introduced in the 17th century. Books
   were bound in crimson morocco, the design consisting of a
   simple three-line gilt panel with an emblem at each corner.

recto
   The right-hand page of an open book; the right-hand side of a sheet
   of paper, as opposed to the verso, the left-hand side.

redact
   Originally, to change the form of something already written,
   as to redact an old play; also, to express appropriately that
   which is expressed inappropriately or in a wrong form, as
   Malory's Le Morte d'Arthur is a redaction of many of the
   Arthurian stories. Today, the term is mainly used to signify:
   to edit or to revise; to prepare for publication.

reduced small
   Paper used for cards measuring two and one-eighth by three
   and one-half inches.

register
   A list of signatures which is often given at the end of early
   books, especially those printed in Italy, which tells the binder
   the order and number of the gatherings in order to assure accuracy. It seems to have been a rare practice in England; also,
   to correspond exactly, as columns or lines of printed matter
   on opposite sheets.

reglet
   A low strip of wood, 6 points (or a multiple thereof up to
   thirty-six points) in thickness, used like leads between lines,
   as in posters, etc.

reissue
   Three main classes: (1) cancellation of title, with or without
   addition, deletion, or substitution of new matter; (2) new impressions, with major part of the work being printed from
   standing type, and resetting is presumed to be by accidental
   distribution; (3) collections.

relief printing
   One of three principal classes of printed illustrations or line.

In this process, a raised printing surface, such as type, wood blocks, halftone plates, etc., are employed. As in letterpress printing, the background is cut away so that only the design takes ink and can be transferred to the paper.

remaindering
The act of a publisher marketing at a reduced price the fag end of an edition to a wholesaler or bookseller for whatever it will bring.

remainders
Copies of a book remaining in the publisher's stock when sales have ceased or become unprofitable.

remboîtage
The transferring of a book from its own binding to another which is more desirable or appropriate.

repoussé
A term sometimes used to describe a design in relief.

reprint
A second or later printing made from the same standing type or plates as the original.

resizing leaves
A weakened paper in an old book is strengthened by dipping in gelatin size. The process is called resizing.

Rheims New Testament
Translated by Cardinal Martin and printed from the Vulgate in 1582 by Fogny. It is the first Roman Catholic English version.

ring (and cup) markings
Whether on rock or stones, they are among the most remarkable of the inscriptions because they are found from Ireland to India possessing the same radical forms.

Riverside Caslon Type
A special printing type designed by Bruce Rogers in the 19th century, based on the original Caslon Type.

roan
 Sheepskin used for bookbinding; generally made of skins that
 are tanned with sumac and colored and finished to imitate
 morocco.

rocker
 A tool used for roughing in the mezzotint process.

roll, parchment
 Parchment is made from the cured hide of a young sheep or
 goat. The hide is scraped clean of hair and fat and then cured
 or tanned to a thin translucent substance; it is then trimmed to
 page size and glued into long rolls. The advantage of the parchment roll over papyrus is that it is more durable in ordinary
 usage and can be more easily written on both sides.

Romains du Roi Type
 A special printing type designed by Philippe Grandjean at the
 order of Louis XIV of France. The Romains du Roi consisted
 in all of eighty-two complete fonts, comprising twenty-one different bodies of roman with twenty different bodies of roman
 capitals, and twenty-one different bodies of italic with twenty
 bodies of italic capitals. The best of the fonts were used in a
 magnificent folio volume illustrating the reign of Louis XIV,
 and published by the Imprimerie Royale in 1702.

Roman alphabet
 The Romans received the alphabet from the Etruscans, who
 had carried the Greek alphabet with them when they migrated
 from the Eastern Mediterranean to Central Italy. In forming
 the Latin alphabet the Romans took over twenty letters of the
 Greek alphabet and added three (G, Y, and Z) of their own.
 Our alphabet is derived from the Latin; to it we have in turn
 added three letters: J, an alternative form of the Latin I;
 U, an alternative form of V; and W, simply two Vs joined
 together.

Roman de la Rose
 One of the outstanding illustrated books published before the
 end of the 15th century.

Roman gems
 Inscriptions have been found on ring stones and other gems.

Even the diamond has not escaped, although inscriptions on it
are very rare because of the difficulty of engraving on it.

Roman hand
A form of the Italian handwriting which has a somewhat upright
character. From it much modern Roman printing is derived.

Roman manuscript production
Very little is known of the actual production of manuscripts
during the Roman Empire, save that it was a flourishing trade
and a profitable business for the publisher; for it was possible
at that time to turn out complete editions of large books cheaply and quickly by employing highly skilled but unpaid slave labor.

Roman Types
Are based on the Neo-Caroline manuscript hand brought into
prominence by the Renaissance scholars. Marked by presence
of curves and lack of "feet." The three main types are: Venetian,
Old French, and Modern.

Rosetta Stone
Its discovery in 1799 represented the first great landmark in
the history of decipherment. The inscription was written, in
196 B.C., in Hieroglyphic, Demotic, and Greek, although part
of the hieroglyphic version had been lost. Prior to the discovery
of the Rosetta Stone, neither Egyptain script nor the Egyptian
language was known to the early discoverers in the seventeenth
century. Found near Rosetta, Egypt, it supplied Champollion
with the key to the ancient inscriptions of Egypt.

rotary press
A cylinder press with the type form curved to fit a rotating
cylinder. The first patent for a machine capable of effecting
an impression from a revolving cylinder upon a curved forme
fastened to the surface of a second revolving cylinder, the
sheet of paper passing between the two in much the same way
as clothes pass through a wringer, was taken out by William
Nicholson of London in 1790. The first actual construction of
a rotary press took place in 1813. But a really successful
machine was not evolved until 1866, this by Walter Press,
used for printing The Times.

rotogravure
> A process of printing in which the impression is produced by etched cylindrical plates affixed to the rollers of a rotary printing press; hence, an illustration so printed.

Rotunda Types
> Rounded, simple printing types with short ascenders and descenders. Used in the 14th century, but soon superseded by the roman types.

rounce of the press
> The handle which, when turned, caused the plank to run between the cheeks of the press.

rounded backing
> The rounded back of the bookbinding which prevents the back from falling in and allows the book to open freely.

rounding, process of
> Rounding is carried out with a hammer, the book being laid on a firm surface and tapped with the hammer until it assumes the correct shape, after which it is placed in a press between backing boards and the outer sections are tapped over to form the joint.

royal packet
> Paper measuring six by nine and one-half inches.

royal pr
> Printing paper measuring twenty by twenty-five inches.

royal, wr
> Writing paper measuring nineteen by twenty-four inches.

rubric
> In early books and manuscripts, a chapter, heading, initial, letter, specific sentence, etc., written or printed in red decorative lettering.

rubrication
> The plain painting of capital letters (the large initials of chapters) in red and blue. When done in silver or gold, the process was called "illumination"; a combination of the two methods

was used for the miniature painting of scenes in the book.

rubricator
One who rubricates or illuminates books, etc.; especially, a member of the medieval brotherhood who added the illuminations, initial letters, etc., to works produced in the monastery.

rule
A strip of brass or steel, type-high, which prints as a line and is named according to its face or use.

rune
Any of the characters or signs of the alphabet formerly in general use from about the 3rd century A.D. among the Teutonic or Germanic peoples. Their origin is obscure, but probably derive from both Latin and Greek. Runes were employed as magic signs and, in writing, as forms of secret communication. They are found in several Anglo-Saxon manuscripts, and in a number of inscriptions, notably Bewcastle cross, Cumberland, England; and the Ruthwell cross, Dumfries, Scotland.

Rune Staves
Wooden rods or flat pieces of wood or other materials containing almanac inscriptions and dating from ancient times; they are of Danish or of Swedish origin. Also called Prime staves, Messe dag staves, Rune stocks, or Brim stocks.

running title
A line of type consisting of the title of the book or the section of the book, found on every page or "opening"; also called running head.

Russia leather
Calf prepared with willow bark and scented with birch oil. It is generally diced, that is, covered all over with diagonal rulings. A modern leather, it wears poorly.

Rustic Capital
A writing style prominent from the second to the fifth century A.D. It was freer, thinner, and more closely compressed than the Quadrata.

Ryland Library
    Erected at Manchester in 1899, it was founded by Mrs. Rylands
    in memory of her husband, a Manchester manufacturer. Within
    thirty-five years of its existence, it grew to 400,000 printed books
    and 12,000 manuscripts, all scholarly books dealing with history
    and literature in their widest sense. The average rate of growth
    has been 10,000 volumes a year.

# S

St. Cuthbert's Gospels
    One of the most curious English bindings. It is a copy of the
    Gospel of St. John, said to have been buried with St. Cuthbert
    at Lindisfarne in the seventh century. It dates from the tenth
    century and is the earliest example of decorative binding.

sand casting
    A casting made in a mold of sand, a method which was ap-
    parently practicable, although it must have been difficult.

sans serif types
    Conform to many of the requirements of good fonts: they ad-
    here to essential alphabet forms, display no attempts at adorn-
    ment, and are evidently expressive of directness and simplic-
    ity. Used for chapter headings, they are pleasingly sharp and
    legible; used for whole books, they are tiresome and illegible.

satin bindings
    Of the fabrics used for binding, satin was one of the more
    popular, the embroidered style being particularly current
    during the reign of Elizabeth. Embroidered satin bindings,
    in a form of split-stitch work, reached a degree of acceptance
    during the 15th century.

sawing-in
A special kind of sewing on cords in order to make a flat spine of the book.

Schwabacher Type
A form of Bastarda printing type.

Scotland, early printing in
Printing was introduced in Scotland in 1508, eleven popular Scottish and English romances being among the earliest works printed, seven of them in 1508.

Scottish bindings
These featured a broad-tooled border, with a centerpiece consisting of a straight stem with short sprays branching from either side at regular intervals.

screen, cross-line
Formed of two plates of glass, each ruled diagonally with a diamond and fastened together at right angles to form a mesh. By means of it, anything which can be photographed can be reproduced by means of a halftone block, taken either from a photograph or painting or other picture and, if necessary, directly from the object.

screen, cross-line process
The screen is placed in the camera in front of the negative. With it in place, the image formed by the lens is broken up by the mesh of the screen into thousands of small cones of light, strongest where the original is lightest.

screw. See spindle and platen.

screw press
A press having a ram that is forced downward by the turning of a spindle having a steep-pitched thread. In common use in the 15th century in every prosperous household, where it was used for the purpose of setting damp domestic linens under pressure to dry. Also common were modifications of it, to make it more suitable for producing impressions from wood blocks or types.

scrinia
Cylindrical boxes in which rolled manuscripts were kept.

script faces
Come in every conceivable variety, some graceful and delicate, others quite repulsive. Among the more beautiful are Madonna Ronde, Bernhard Tango, and Trafton; among the less attractive are Holla, Fanal, Penflow, and Pentape.

scriptoria, monastic
Writing rooms in the monasteries in which the production of fine manuscripts took place. They were out of bounds to every-one except the scribes and the higher monastic officers. All work done in the scriptoria was under the supervision of a senior monk known as the Armarius.

Scriptorum Brytannie Catalogus
First English attempt at a national bibliography was prepared by a penniless Bishop Bales and printed at Basle (because of official bigotry at home) in 1557-1559.

secondary binding
Publishers seldom bind at one time all the copies printed. In-stead, they order bindings as the demand for the books arise. Hence a slow-selling book may be bound in batches over a period of years and variant bindings result. The first binding is the primary one; the others are secondary.

Secretary Hand
The ordinary writing of the sixteenth century in England--the hand that Shakespeare wrote; also known as the English Hand.

semis
Small figures (sawings of a single small tool) used to cover free spaces in bookbinding designs.

sepia
Ink derived from the black fluid ejected by the cuttlefish.

serif
One of the fine lines of a letter, especially one of the fine cross strokes at the top or bottom.

set-wise measurement
Type sizes are measured in points, a point equalling .013837 inch, with the measurement taken from the belly of the type to

the back. The measurement is accurate in reference to the tail of the longest descender and the top of the longest ascender; but it does not reliably indicate the x-height, which is the size of the letter x and other letters such as a, e, r, w, etc., that have neither ascender nor descender. It is by these letters that the apparent size of type is judged; and in different faces they are not in the same proportion to the ascenders and the descenders.

sewing, French
There is an increasing tendency to omit tapes in sewn books. Books without tapes are described as French sewn.

sewing machine in bookbinding
A section of a book is opened at the middle and laid astride a metal saddle, which then conveys it to a set of needles in the upper part of the machine, where the section is pierced and sewn through with thread. Other sections are laid one by one in the same way and sewn to the previous one, with lengths of tape, during the operation, being laced in with the stitches across the spine. In this way, several copies of the book are sewn together and must be cut apart before the following stage begins.

Shakespeare Press
Its primary purpose was to publish an edition of Shakespeare's works illustrated from the Shakespearian drawings in John Boydell's Pall Mall Gallery.

sheet
A rectangular piece of paper which is cut to a definite and uniform size for the printing of books and other publications.

sheet and half cap
Size measuring thirteen and one-half by twenty-four and one-half inches.

sheet and half demy
Size measuring twenty-two and one-half by twenty-six and one-half inches.

sheet and half foolscap
Size measuring thirteen and one-quarter by twenty-four and one-half inches.

sheet and half post
Size measuring nineteen and one-half by twenty-three and one-half inches.

sheet and third foolscap
Size measuring thirteen and one-quarter by twenty-two inches.

sheet sizes in English book papers
The common sizes, in open sheets, are:
crown, twenty by fifteen inches;
demy, twenty and one-half by seventeen and one-half inches;
imperial, thirty by twenty-two inches;
large foolscap, seventeen by thirteen and one-half inches;
large post, twenty-one by sixteen and one-half inches;
large royal, twenty-seven by twenty inches;
medium, twenty-three by eighteen inches;
royal, twenty-five by twenty inches.

Sholes Typewriter Patent
Although the first American patent was taken out in Detroit by Burt in 1823, the first practical typewriter was invented at Milwaukee in 1867 by Sholes, Glidden, and Soule.

short demy
Size of paper measuring fourteen and three-eights by twenty and three-quarters inches

shoulder heads
Cross heads are centered across (or in the middle of) the line, with one or two lines of space above them and perhaps half a line below. Shoulder heads are subsidiary to side heads, and the type used for them should align and work with the text type without discomfort or trouble. Generally in capitals, shoulder heads are in a normal position the opening words of the paragraph. Cut-in heads are not often met with, but can be effective if properly used. The marginal head is placed in the foredge margin at the level required. It should be set in a style of type that prevents its being confused with the text type.

side heads
Are subsidiary to cross heads (see above) and are almost as flexible in variety of emphasis. The lines of space above are generally twice as many as the lines below them.

sigillography
A special literature on a subdivision of diplomatics (the science of medieval documents); specifically, the department of learning dealing with seals.

sigla
In the fifteenth and sixteenth centuries, single letters were used as abbreviations for words and names: thus .H. meant "Henry"; .L. meant "Lord" or "Lordship"; .i. meant id est; .s. meant scilicet, and so forth. Such abbreviations were called sigla (sigles), from the Latin word sigillum (a seal).

signature
A letter or other mark found at the bottom of the first leaf of each gathering, which serves as a guide to the binder in placing the sheets in their proper order. As far as binding is concerned, the signature is deemed more reliable than page numbers. The form varies, but examples are A or Ai, Aij; or $A_1$, $A_2$, $A_3$, etc.

silk and silver bindings
The ornamentation of book covers dates from antiquity. Extant examples include ivory diptychs of the third century and book covers of the fifth century, with bindings being in gold, silver, and jewels and, toward the close of the Middle Ages, in velvet and silk.

Sinaitic inscriptions
It is clear that there existed in Sinai (that is, on Semitic soil), not later than 1500 B.C., a form of writing almost certainly alphabetic in character and clearly based upon the Egyptian hieroglyphics.

sixty-fourmo
A book composed of sheets each of which is folded into sixty-four leaves; usually written 64mo.

size
Any thin, pasty substance, usually an animal gelatin, used for filling in the pores in the surface of paper, fiber, etc., or, in bookbinding, for applying color, metal, or ink leaf to book edges or covers.

size of books. See format.

size of type. See point system.

sizing
   The process of making paper nonabsorbent, so that it will take
   ink without blurring.

skins as writing material
   Used from the very beginning, with, of course, some improvement in the preparation of the surface. There is a story that
   when King Ptolemy of Egypt, because of jealousy of a rival book
   collector King Attalus of Pergamun, placed an embargo on
   papyrus, King Attalus resorted to the use of skins as writing
   material. From Pergamum comes the name pergamene or
   parchment (sheepskin or goatskin), which we loosely inter-
   change with vellum (calfskin). Our oldest extant Greek parchment dates from the early second century.

skiver
   A soft, thin leather made of the grain of a split sheepskin,
   tanned in sumac, dyed, and used for bookbinding, especially
   for pocket books. It looks well for the moment, but it is not
   so strong as good paper. (The remaining part of the split
   sheepskin is treated differently and made into chamois leather.)

slip proof
   Same as galley proof.

slips
   When all the sections of a work are sewn by the binder, the
   cords are cut, leaving a short length projecting at each side;
   these ends are called slips and are used later in attaching the
   book to its boards.

The Sloane Collection
   Very impressive in botanical and zoological records and drawings, and including substantial Egyptain papyri, valuable
   Oriental MSS., and many Greek and Roman MSS. of lesser
   importance.

slug
   A strip of metal, usually six points (1/12 of an inch) thick, less

than type-high, which is used to space between lines, at the top or bottom of a column, etc.; also, a type-high strip, as one with a figure, letter, or word, for temporary identifying use, or a line of type cast in one piece on a machine.

small atlas, English
Paper measuring twenty-five by thirty-one inches.

small cap.
Paper measuring thirteen by sixteen inches.

small cards
Measure two and one-half by three and one-half inches.

small double cap.
Paper measuring sixteen by twenty-six inches.

small double post
Paper measuring nineteen by twenty-nine inches.

small post
Paper measuring thirteen and one-half by sixteen and one-half inches.

smasher
An automatic machine or clamp, capable of some hundred pounds of pressure, into which books are fed in stacks at one end and delivered at the other properly consolated and compacted ("smashed, bumped, or nipped").

soft-ground etching
Differs from ordinary etching in that the ground is softened by mixture with tallow and the design drawn with a pencil on a sheet of paper laid over the ground; also, an impression on paper, parchment, etc., taken in ink from an etched plate. In the process of etching, the etcher covers his plate with a soft granulated ground and draws on the paper laid over it. The pressure of the needle makes the waxy ground on the lines adhere to the paper, which lifts it when raised, but does not leave the lines clean, a certain amount of the ground remaining. The acid bites irregularly around these grains, and the line that results is composed of flecks.

Solus Type
>One of the special printing types designed by Eric Gill, an outstanding type designer (1882-1940).

Sonatas of III Parts
>Appearance in 1683 of Purcell's work marks probably the first book by Cross, regarded as the greatest music engraver in England, if not in all of Europe. Cross' work laid the foundations in any country for mass production of music publications.

sorts
>The pieces of type which belong to one font.

space
>A small piece of type used to separate words (or letters) in a line of type. It is cast lower than the face of the type, so as not to receive the ink in printing, and is usually made in three widths, 3-ems (three to an em), 4-ems, and 5-ems. Also, in composition, to increase the spaces between words so as to fill a line; to extend the length of a page or job by inserting leads or furniture; to blank out, as with quads or furniture.

space, hair
>Thinner than a 5-em space.

space, justifying
>One which is automatically cast on the monotype machine between the words, of such width that, with other similar spaces, it will fill out the line of type in which it occurs.

spacing
>The gaps or spaces between each word in an arrangement of words on a typed page; also the gaps between lines or paragraphs on a typed page.

special bibliographies
>Not limited to country or language, or subject; concerned with special categories.

sphragistics
>The science of seals, their history, age, distinctions, etc.

spindle

The screw which regulates the bar of the hand press relative
to the amount of pressure that is to be exerted on the forme.

spine

The back of the book which shows when it is shelved. It is
ordinarily differentiated as follows: the flexible spine, freely
moving without yielding to the stress placed upon it; the fast
spine, which does not bend with the opening of the book; the
hollow spine, which is separate from the spine of the cover,
so that while the first bends, the second retains its shape.

spiral back binding

Metal or plastic spirals, generally used for books that are
to be opened absolutely flat.

spray wax

Used to bathe each sheet immediately after impression to form
an impervious layer over the ink to prevent set-off.

stabbing

Binding pages together in book form by lacing a cord through
holes pierced sideways through the entire thickness of the back
of the book, as in making Orihons.

stamps

The major part of the design on the leather bindings of books,
distinguished from the smaller work of "tooling."

standards

The punches of a type font that are made first and serve as a
dimensional and design models for other letters.

Stanhope Press

Invented by Charles Mahon, 3rd Earl Stanhope, in the year
1800, it was the first major improvement upon the hand press.
Its frame was no longer made of wood, but cast as a single
piece of iron. The platen was still operated by means of a
screw, but this had a series of levers added to it which facil-
itated the operation required to obtain a satisfactory impression.

stapling
>The process of binding in which wire clips or staples are used in place of sewing.

Star Chamber Decree of 1586
>Strengthened state control of printing by asserting that all existing and future presses were to be notified to the Master and Wardens of the Stationers' Company and by prohibiting all printing outside of London and the universities of Oxford and Cambridge, the latter being limited to one press each.

Star Chamber Decree of 1637
>Reduced the total number of printers in England to twenty-three: the King's Printer, twenty London printers, and one printer each at the universities of Oxford and Cambridge.

stationer
>Specifically, a publishing bookseller or publisher registered with the Company of Stationers, as distinct from an itinerant vendor; so called from his occupying a station in the market-place or elsewhere. Loosely, a bookseller or publisher, or one who sells books or other articles used in writing.

The Stationers' Company
>One of the Livery Companies of the City of London founded in 1556, comprising booksellers, bookbinders, and dealers in writing materials. The official Charter of Incorporation was granted by Mary in 1557 and confirmed by Elizabeth in 1559. In 1560 the Company was formally created one of the Livery Companies of the City of London. Although the Charter of Incorporation granted by Mary in 1557 was given in response to a petition by the members of the Company itself, it was clear from the start that the Crown meant to use the Company as a means of censorship and of restraining the production and distribution of seditious literature within the realm. To effect this objective, the master and wardens of the Company were given wide powers to search the buildings of any printer or bookseller, and to confiscate or burn any illegal or seditious works which were possessed or published by them.

Stationers' Hall
>The hall of the guild of stationers (i.e., booksellers or publishers) of London, now near Ludgate Hill. This guild for nearly

three hundred years regulated the publication of all books in England. From 1842 to 1911, under the copyright law, registration at Stationers' Hall, although not compulsory, was necessary before taking proceedings relative to infringement of copyright.

stechometry
The enumeration of the number of letters, words, and lines in the original edition specified in the copy, to protect the buyer from omissions and interpolations.

steel engraving
The art or process of engraving on steel, rather than on copper; an impression taken from a steel plate. Steel engraving produces a very delicate line and makes for a beautiful illustration. It was very popular in the nineteenth century.

stencil
The earliest method of applying color to book illustration, apart from hand painting in gold and colors, was by means of watercolor and stencils. Stencils were extensively used in the production of the Helgen and early playing cards and, after the introduction of printing, as a semi-mechanical method of coloring the outline woodcuts by means of which early books were illustrated.

stenography, early examples of
The earliest examples of Greek shorthand (papyri of second and third centuries) still remain undeciphered. Papyri belonging to the fourth to the eighth centuries and another group belonging to the tenth century evidence the use of shorthand, but are only slightly superior to ordinary writing in the matter of speed and economy of space.

stereotype
A method of reproducing as one single typographic unit from an original surface locked up in a forme and composed of separate type characters and illustrative blocks. The plate is made by taking a mold or matrix of a printing surface in plaster of Paris, paper pulp, or the like, and making from this a cast in type metal, often with more than the usual percentage of lead. Today stereotypes are used mainly for newspaper work;

books are usually electrotyped, the surface of an electrotype being more durable. When stereotypes are used for magazine or book printing, they are nickel plated to increase their durability.

stick
In the process of setting type, it is the shallow tray with a handle used to hold type.

stipple
A method of engraving in which the effect is produced by dots. The plate is first covered with an ordinary etching ground, through which the contours and a light indication of the main shadows are dotted by means of etching needles or a roulette. The uncovered portions are bitten with acid and the subject is then given brilliance by flicking or dotting directly on to the surface of the plate with a specially curved graver or a roulette.

stitches, kettle
Special stitches used by the binder to attach sections at head and tail before cutting the cords.

stone
A stand or table with a smooth flat top, originally of stone, but now often of metal, on which to impose type.

stone-hand
The individual who imposes the pages of type, derived from the fact that the imposing surface or table was originally made of stone.

stop-cylinder press
Cylinder presses are of two kinds: one, in which the type bed remains static, while the impression cylinder rolls over it; another, in which the bed moves to and fro under the cylinder which imparts the impression as the two move in unison. The stop-cylinder press belongs to the second type. It has a single large cylinder which revolves once for every sheet printed. Also called Wharfedale, from the valley of the River Wharfe, where most presses of this kind are made.

Stowe Missal
An 11th-century manuscript from Tipperary, Ireland, famous for its decorated Cumdach or book box.

straight grain
>An exaggeration of the natural grain of morocco causing it to resemble a ploughed field.

Strawberry Hill Press
>The first English private press of any size to remain in operation over a number of years (1757 to 1797). It was founded by Sir Horace Walpole, 4th Earl of Oxford. Much of its work was good, but little of it after 1789.

stubbing
>Narrow strips of paper sewed in albums or sample books to allow for tip-ins.

stuff
>The pulp from which papers may be manufactured.

stuff chest
>A large vat or reservoir, in which the pulp is kept constantly in motion, to prevent the fibers from settling until ready for use.

style of type, indications of
>A waved line indicates that the matter is to be printed in bold or black face; a single straight line indicates italics, etc.

stylus
>A hard pointed piece or instrument, of wood, ivory, glass, or metal, used, in early times, for writing on wax; today used to trace or write on carbon paper so as to make impressions on the paper beneath the carbon.

subheads
>Means by which chapters are divided into sections. They may be set in a number of different ways and in different types, provided they blend with the general style of the book. There are five main varieties:

>cross heads   Centered across the measure, with one or more lines of space above them and perhaps half a line below.

>cut-in heads   They can be useful, if well employed, but they are more difficult to set and more expensive than other subheads.

marginal heads   Generally placed in foredge margin at desired level, they should be set in a style that differentiates them from text type.

shoulder heads   Subsidiary to side heads, they do not normally provide much emphasis and are as a rule set in the same size type as the text.

side heads   Subsidiary to cross heads and almost as flexible in variety of emphasis, with spaces above and below, as a cross head, or only above.

Subiaco Type
A special type designed by H. St. John Hornby and used at the Ashendene Press. The De Divinis Institutionibus was the first book to contain passages printed in Greek type. The fourth and last book printed at Subiaco was St. Augustine's Civitas Dei, published in 1467.

subject bibliography
Limited to the consideration of certain motifs or topics of interest.

subject catalogue
A catalogue in which books, etc., are listed only under the subjects treated, arranged alphabetically or by classes.

subject concepts
Form the borderline between entry-word concepts and actual concepts. They consist of concepts which are differentiated and limited by topic or subject matter.

sunk panel bindings
Practiced by the Moors and introduced by them into Venice in the second half of the 15th century. Two boards were used for each cover, one of them being cut out in panels and laid over the other. They were then covered with thinly pared leather which was worked down until it took on the form of the sunken panels. The leather was then either painted or ornamented in blind or gilt.

superroyal, boards
Measures twenty-one and one-half by twenty-nine inches.

superroyal, dr.
Drawing paper measuring nineteen by twenty-seven inches.

superroyal, Eng.
Paper size in England measuring nineteen by twenty-seven inches.

superroyal, pr.
Paper used in printing measuring twenty and one-half by twenty-seven and one-half inches.

superroyal, wr. U.S.
Writing paper, used in America, measuring twenty by twenty-eight inches.

surface paper
A paper sized, calendered, or otherwise surfaced.

surface printing
Printing, by any process, as the lithographic or gelatin process, which employs a plane printing surface. See intaglio and relief printing.

swash letters
A more script-like ornamental font of italic type.

syllabic writing
The evolutionary stages of writing are generally believed to be: (1) pictures; (2) pictographs, conventionalized pictures emphasizing the distinguishing detail (e.g., astronomical signs); (3) ideographs, symbols representing the idea, rather than the object (e.g., arrow pointing direction, Indian in front of cigar store); (4) phonogram, symbol representing the sound, rather than the realistic object or its idea; (5) a combination of phonogram and rebus (similar to our game of charades); (6) the simplification of the rebus-phonogram to syllables; (7) simplification of the rebus-phonogram to alphabetical sounds (the principle of "acrophony").

# T

Tablet of Sen
 An inscribed stone similar to the Rosetta Stone, but of an earlier
 date (238 B.C.). It contains a decree of the priests at Canopus in
 honor of Ptolemy Evergetes I.

tabulae
 Thin, oblong-shaped sheets of wood covered with wax and having a
 raised edge all around to prevent the sheets from adhering and so
 obliterating the writing.

tail
 The lower margin of the leaf (the bottom of the page); also, the
 foot of the backstrip.

tailpiece
 An ornament for a blank space at the foot of a page, most usually at the end of a chapter or poem.

tall copy
 An especially good copy of a book, with ample margins at the
 tops and bottoms of the pages; also, the name given to a book
 which is said to be uncut, that is, not reduced in size by having
 been rebound (valuable).

term catalogue
 Lists books in print; first appeared in 1668.

tests of books of reference or information
 Fitness or relevancy of subject matter; range or scope;
 treatment (quality or level of); authority; date; arrangement;
 format.

Textura Type
 A form of Gothic type, with short ascenders and descenders
 ending in points known as "feet." Compressed on the page,
 Textura types make the printed matter resemble a woven
 texture; hence the name. Used by Gutenberg and his associates.
 The English equivalent was called Block Letter.

theorem
A drawing paper measuring twenty-eight by thirty-four inches.

thick-paper copies
Seventeenth and eighteenth-century books which were printed
on a superior fine paper (usually Dutch), today occasionally
referred to as thick-paper copies.

three-color process
The principle of the three-color theory was actually discovered
by J. C. Bolon (1667-1741), who declared that all gradations of
color could be produced from the three primary colors--red,
blue, and yellow. The process is as follows: the original article is photographed three times: once with a violet filter, then
with a green filter, and thirdly with an orange filter. The fil-
ters divide the colors of the original into three main photographic
divisions--yellow, red, and blue respectively. Each photo is
taken on negative material and the resultant three negatives are
known as "color separation negatives." From these, three plates
are prepared and, when these are next inked in yellow, red, and
blue inks and printed from successively in register, the resultant
print produces accurately the full range of colors in the original
article or picture.

three-quarter binding
The leather covers the spine and one-third of each cover; or,
as half bound, but with wider leather back and corners.

ties
Tapes or ribbons which are slotted into the sides of a binding
near the outer edge; when tied, they prevent the covers from
warping or gaping. No longer used (generally) since about the
middle of the 17th century.

tight back
A backbone which adheres solidly to the cover.

till
A cross piece between the cheeks of the hand press which served
as a guide to keep the motion of the spindle exactly vertical.

tipping in
The practice in binding of pasting the edge of a single leaf to the next leaf, usually to insert plates or errata slips.

tissues
They are tipped in or loosely inserted beside illustrations, for example, to absorb offset or, on occasion, for decoration.

title, bastard
An abbreviated title which precedes the full title page; loosely, a half title.

title, half
The name of a book placed at the head of the first page of text; or, a title, as of a subdivision, standing alone on a page introducing the subdivision. Also signifies any part of the title that occupies a page of itself.

title page
A separate page giving the title of the book and not containing any part of the text itself. It was seldom used in MS., although knowledge of it preceded its introduction in printed books. The equivalent page in manuscripts was designed apparently for embellishment than to describe contents. Stages in the development of the title page were:
(1) During the sixteenth and seventeenth centuries, the title page was an explanatory label affixed to the work by the printer or publisher, rather than a production of the author. It listed the contents, but not the author's name. In time, it took over the function of the colophon, containing the first date of printing, the sign of the printer or bookseller, and, towards the end of the period, including praises of the work and author.
(2) After the Restoration, the title page became more factual, listing the title itself, the author's name, the printer and publisher, and the date of publication.
(3) In the later eighteenth century, the title page began to include mention of the earlier works of the author.

title page, the evolution of its form
At first only the title was given, in a type style not much different from that of the text. Between 1520 and 1560, the woodcut title page border became popular and, towards the end of

the sixteenth century, plain horizontal rules were introduced, sometimes above the title, sometimes below it; and occasionally the page was divided into two or three panels. By the end of the seventeenth century, woodcut borders had virtually disappeared, the rule border now dividing the page into panels. The eighteenth-century title page tended toward greater simplicity, with vignettes frequently appearing in the center of the page. The experiments conducted in the nineteenth century related mainly to arrangement.

title page, treatment of
Should be dignified, yet suitable to nature of work and in keeping with the rest of the layout.

toe
A cylindrical portion of the press below the bar, which worked in a depression on the upper surface of the platen.

tooling
The binder's tools are the engraved metal implements (usually of brass) which he uses to impress designs on the covers of books; such as rolls, fillets, pallets, gouges. Hence to tool is to letter or ornament (for example, a book cover) in blind impression, or in gold, silver, etc., by means of heated hand tools. First known in the eighth century.

trade binding
Books which were bound in the seventeenth and eighteenth centuries before issue by the retail or wholesale booksellers, the bibliographical equivalent of the publisher's bindings of the modern period.

transcript
A written or printed copy of an original holograph, as when a writer writes out a favorite piece for a friend or an admirer; the result (although an autograph) is a transcript, not an original manuscript in the strict sense.

Treacle Bible
Cloverdale's translation, produced in black letter in 1535 at Zurich, is the first whole Bible printed in English.

treatise
> A book or article which treats a subject, especially in a sys-
> tematic manner, for an expository or argumentative purpose.

tree-calf binding
> Made from the sides of a calf which have been stained by the
> interaction of copperas and pearl-ash to a design resembling
> a tree and then highly polished; popular in the nineteenth century.

trial binding
> Samples of proposed covers for books have from early times
> been submitted from binder to publisher and, occasionally, from
> publisher to author. In modern times, the samples are "dummies,"
> mainly if not entirely made up of blank leaves; but in the nine-
> teenth century finished copies were sometimes used. Authentic
> trial bindings are prized by collectors.

trial edition
> In rare instances, usually at the request of authors, a work
> was set up in type at an early stage and some copies printed for
> circulation among friends or for the author's convenience in
> revision. It became a trial edition if the work was subsequent-
> ly reset before being printed for publication. It otherwise re-
> mained a trial issue.

trichromatic halftone process
> A color reproduction process in which yellow, red, and blue
> are printed on top of one another to represent all colors.

trimmed
> When differentiated, as occasionally they are, the word cut
> means that the edges of a book's leaves have been cut smooth,
> whereas trimmed means that they have been more roughly
> levelled. More commonly employed for the latter is the ex-
> pression rough-trimmed.

tub sizing
> Passing the paper through a tub or vat containing a sizing
> solution as of gelatin or starch to give a coating.

two-revolution machine
> Differs from the stop-cylinder press in that the cylinder does
> not stop when the bed returns on the non-printing stroke, but
> continues to revolve.

tympan
> An iron frame covered with a sheet of parchment or thick paper, upon which the sheet of paper to be printed was placed. This was turned over and brought down upon the type.

type
> A raised rectangular solid or prism of metal, wood, and other hard material having a raised letter, figure, or punctuation mark or other characters on the upper end which, when inked, is used to make impressions on paper and other smooth surfaces. The main parts of a type are: (1) body or shank, the rectangular solid itself; (2) shoulder, the part of the end of the body unoccupied by face; (3) face, the raised letters or characters; (4) nicks, notches made on one side of the prism and designed to help the compositor in distinguishing the bottom from the top; (5) groove, a channel made at the bottom or foot of the type to make it stand steadily.

typecase. See case.

typefaces, basic divisions
> Book faces, characters used for book text; jobbing faces, characters suitable for display; poster faces, characters suitable for placards.

typefaces for display
> At first display types differed from regular typefaces only in size; but after about 1700, they began to assume varied shapes, for example, of branches and twigs.

type founder
> The craftsman who casts type.

type foundry
> The establishment concerned with the design and production of metal printing type for hand composition.

type measurement in early times
> The arbitrary unit of depth is twenty lines. Hence 78R signifies that the book is printed in roman type, twenty lines of which measure seventy-eight millimeters in depth.

type measurement in modern times
> System now in use in America was adopted in 1886 by the United States Type Founders' Association, although many founders were already using it. It is based upon a French system using the pica body as the unit of reference. This body is divided into twelfths, called "points," and every type body consists of a given number of these points. The value of the point is .013837 inch or nearly 1/72 inch.

type punch
> A hard metal tool, driven into the end of a matrix blank, so as to produce there a corresponding letter cavity. In the early stages of printing, this probably was the mechanical process used to fabricate matrices.

typescripts, three kinds of
> (a) Author's original typescript, the original manuscript or first autograph draft; (b) author's fair copy typescript, an autograph manuscript fair copy; (c) copyist's typescript, a fair copy written other than by the author.

type specimen sheets
> Generally issued by typefounder to the printers who buy type; or by printers to publishers who buy printing.

Typograph
> Like the Linotype, it is a typecasting, setting, and distributing machine; it differs from the Linotype in its mechanism.

typographer
> In simplest terms, the man who designs or arranges printing, a compositor. More precisely, in today's use, the individual who uses type as the material of his design: he is to the book what the architect is to the building, the integrator of the many diverse trades involved in the production of a book.

typographic data
> Information which is in any way related to the technical preparation of the book: orthography, selection of type, method of reproduction, styles of illustration--all the material of which the book is made.

typography
> Art of printing with type; use of type to produce impressions on paper, vellum, etc.; also, the style, arrangement, or appearance of the matter printed from type.

typolithography
> A branch of lithography in which impressions from printers' types are transferred to stone for reproduction.

# U

umbilicus
> The stick upon which a papyrus manuscript was rolled, to which the last sheet was attached; also, an ornamental knob, button, or boss, at the ends of such a stick.

unauthorized edition. See authorized edition; piracy, literary.

uncial script
> A book hand used especially in Greek or Latin manuscripts of the fourth to the eighth centuries A.D., which consisted of somewhat rounded separated majuscules, but with cursive forms for some letters. After the tenth century, the uncial script was superseded by the minuscule hand.

uncut
> A book is said to be uncut if the margins are of the original width, indicating that the book has not been reduced in size by having been rebound.

union catalogue
> A catalogue which combines in one series a number of catalogues, or the contents of more than one library.

unique copy
    A manuscript or an autograph letter or drawing is of course
    unique. A book with an inscription or annotation, not likely to
    have been repeated in any other copy, is also unique.

unlettered copy
    One which does not have a title or author's name on the spine
    of the binding; usual in books of the sixteenth and first half of
    the seventeenth centuries.

unopened
    A book in which the leaves have not been cut apart is described
    as unopened. In the case of an uncut book, the binder's intention
    is to retain the original margins (and hence deckle edges); in
    the case of an unopened book, the binder's intention is to cut the
    leaves but, for one reason or another, he has failed to do so.

unpressed book
    One which has not been in the binder's press, as a result of which
    the paper preserves its original briskness of texture.

unsewn binding
    The fixing of single leaves to each other by means of a rubber
    solution. The leaves are brought together and the spine is
    roughened and coated with India rubber; while the solution is
    still sticky, a backing is put on, followed by boards.

upper case
    The top one of a pair of compositor's cases, containing capital
    letters; the capital letter itself.

uterine vellum
    The finest of all vellums, made of the skin of the unborn (or
    stillborn) calf; used for illuminated manuscripts.

# V

variants

Copies in a single issue that differ because the corrections were made while the issue was still being printed, so that some copies are amended, others are not. All are of the same issue, however.

variorium edition

An edition of the author's work presenting complete variant readings of the possible texts and full notes of the critical comments and interpretations passed upon the text by major writers.

Vatican Library

Founded by Pope Nicholas V in 1447, it is today one of the most accessible and valuable literary institutions in Europe. Its collections include some 60,000 manuscripts and 7000 incunabula.

vatman

Operator of a mold for making paper.

vellum

Originally, prepared from the skin of calf (not split) for writing upon. Used as early as 197-182 B.C. Prepared well, it provides a very smooth and brilliant surface to write upon. Still used by calligraphers today and in the production of fine printings. In medieval times, most manuscripts were written on vellum.

vellum bindings

Limp vellum or limp parchment was commonly used in the sixteenth and seventeenth centuries for binding, often plain, sometimes decorated in gilt. In more recent times it has been used much like leather, as covering for board sides.

Venetian Type

First cut in 1470 by Nicolas Jenson, a Frenchman working in Venice; characterized by heavy slab serifs, thick main strokes, and slightly round forms. It is still regarded as one of the most beautiful and legible of all types.

**verso**
> The back or reverse side of the leaf, the left-hand side of an open book (opposed to <u>recto</u>, the right-hand side of an open book).

**vignette**
> A relatively small decorative design or illustration of any kind put on, or just before, the title page, or used as a headpiece or tailpiece to a chapter or division of a book or, in earlier times, a manuscript; any picture which shades off gradually into the surrounding ground of the unprinted paper.

**Visigothic Handwriting**
> Roman cursive hand as written in Spain, where it was affected by Spanish national characteristics.

**<u>volumen</u>**
> The Latin word for <u>roll</u>, usually employed in reference to rolled manuscripts; from this derives the modern word <u>volume</u>.

**Vulgate Bible**
> St. Jerome translated the Bible from Hebrew and Greek into Latin 383-405 A.D. By 800 A.D. it had superseded all earlier translations of the Bible. It is the text printed by Gutenberg in 1456, the earliest date that can positively be assigned to any printed book. Known as the Vulgate, it was declared by the Council of Trent in 1546 to be the standard for the services of the Catholic Roman Church. It is extant in no less than 8000 manuscripts.

# W

**wampum**
> Beads made of shells, used by the North American Indians as money, as ceremonial pledges, or as ornaments. They were polished and strung together in strands, belts, or sashes.

wampum belt
> Used as a mnemonic device or ceremonially, especially in the ratification of treatises. Used also as money.

washed
> The reference is to the washing of leaves and complete volumes, especially by the French, in a chemical solution for the purpose of taking out spots, stains, and other blemishes. Since the washing also removes size from the paper, the leaves (or book) must then be given a size bath.

waste
> Spoiled or surplus sheets of printed matter used, in earlier days, for making up boards or for endpapers.

waterleaf
> Handmade paper in its initial stage of manufacture, consisting of pulp spread and evened by shaking in the hand mold, and pressed between felts. To give it a non-absorbent quality, or a surface that will take ink without blurring, the paper, at this point, is sized by being dipped into a solution of animal gelatin.

watermark
> The distinguishing mark of the paper manufacturer, made by interweaving a design in wire in the network of cross wires in the mold. When the paper is held up to the light, the impression of the wires appears as semi-transparent lines. The designs ranged from simple stars, crosses, and initials to elaborate heraldic arms, jugs, pillars, and crowns. The watermark was usually placed in the center of one half of the sheet, but in the sixteenth and seventeenth centuries, it sometimes is found elsewhere. Watermarks first appeared in Western papers of the thirteenth century. They are normal in laid paper, abnormal in wove paper. They provide valuable evidence of the make-up of a book and have proved helpful pointers to the existence of a cancel or the clever insertion of an alien leaf. They are especially useful for books through the eighteenth century.

wax tablets
> A thin film of wax, usually black or green, was spread upon a hard white surface (hence the word <u>album</u>), usually a thin sheet of wood. Upon this, in antiquity, writing was engraved with a stylus made of metal or bone.

Weekly News from Italy, Germany, etc., The
First English newspaper to appear in London, printed in 1622.

wetting down
The process, in the early stages of printing, of rendering paper softer before the impressions were made on it; a method which compensated for irregularities in size of the typefaces.

white-line engraving. See wood engraving

whole binding
The covering with leather, or other material, of the entire outside of the book--the spine (or back) and the covers.

wholesaler's binding
In the nineteenth century, some booksellers purchased their stock of new books in quires and had them bound in bulk, independently of the publisher. The term is also used as an acceptable synonym for trade binding, relative to eighteenth-century books.

winter of the press
The fourth cross piece on the hand press, a massive piece of timber which supported the type and offered the counter-resistance to the pressure of the screw. It was at the bottom of the cheeks of the press, about two feet, six inches from the ground.

wire-lines or wire-marks
Several lines which run vertically across a page where the paper appears to be thinner than elsewhere, due to the wire bed of the mold in which the paper was made.

Wittenberg Type
A form of Bastarda type.

woodblock
A piece of wood on which lines, letters, or figures are engraved in order to be printed from it, or to be stamped out by pressure from it.

woodblock printing. See xylography.

woodcutting

An early method of illustration. The design is cut in relief upon a block of wood with a special woodcutting knife. The surface is then inked and prints are taken from it by laying paper over it, and rubbing it over the back. The resultant print appears on the paper as a design of black lines on a white background. Hence, woodcutting is also known as black-line method.

wood engraving

In this the illustrator works on the end of a block of hardwood across the grain with a graver instead of a knife. In wood-cutting, the block of wood is planed with the grain, and a knife is used to cut away everything except the portions that are to appear black on the paper. In wood engraving, the resultant print appears on the paper as a design of white line on a black background (hence the white-line method).

wood pulp

It is today the main raw material of paper throughout the world, being generally employed in America in the manufacture of all but the finest grade paper. Wood pulp is of two kinds: mechanical, which is produced by grinding the wood until it is almost sawdust before pulping it by chemical treatment; chemical, which is produced by cutting the wood first into small blocks, about an inch square, and then subjecting it to a chemical process. Chemical wood pulp is used to make paper which has greater strength and does not fade so easily; hence used widely in the production of books.

wormholes

Made in paper, and sometimes in boards and leather bindings, by the bookworm, a maggot. Considered less offensive by the bibliophile than the blemish of dirt or browning.

worms

A name given to the three or four threads in the spindle of the printing press.

wove mold

Consists of an intricately fine mesh of fibers; gives paper the appearance of being woven.

**wove paper**
Paper with even, granulated texture, used for ordinary book
printing since the early nineteenth century; distinguished from
laid or mold-made (handmade) paper. The laid mold consists
of a close mesh of fine wires, running lengthwise and crossed
at intervals of about three-quarters of an inch by stouter wires;
the wove mold is a very fine mesh, closely woven.

**wrapper**
A paper wrapping around a finished book, covering it entirely
and usually having sealed ends; also, the detachable paper
cover put on a book to protect the binding.

**writing ink in early times**
Water in which finely powdered coloring matter was suspended.
A second substance available to the fifteenth-century printer
was thin oil paint.

# X

**Xativa**
The oldest and most important paper mill of Spain.

**x-height**
The size of the letter x and other letters, such as, for example,
a, that is, letters which have neither ascenders nor descenders.

**xylographic**
Of or pertaining to an impression or print made from an artistic
wood carving.

**xylographs**
Single sheet pictures printed from wood blocks, the earliest
dating from 1423; an engraving on wood, or the impression

from such an engraving; a print made by the xylographic process.

xylography
The process in which printing is done from an inked surface formed by cutting on a wooden block the lines of the original design in reverse, and then cutting away the background, so that the raised design is left as the printing surface. In early times, single words only were cut on the wood block; but as the woodcutters became more expert, whole sentences were incorporated.

# Y

yapp
A style of binding in which a limp cover bends over the edges without being bent at the corners, named after Yapp, a London bookseller, for whom a publisher bound Bibles in this style about 1850. In America, called divinity circuit binding.

yapp edges
The rough edges on the paper of the book itself. Of two kinds: (1) soft and floppy; (2) stiff edges that are permanently turned at right angle to the board itself.

yellow-back
Name given to particular type of cheap edition, in the middle of the nineteenth century, of works, usually fiction, which were frequently displayed and sold in railway stations.

# Z

### zincograph

Called zincas in England, the metal plate (zinc) which is etched
and mounted on wood to bring it to the desired type height for
printing; thus, a zinc plate prepared for printing by zincography;
also, a print from such a plate.

### zincography

The art or process of putting designs of any kind in the form
of a printing surface on zinc plates, and of producing impressions therefrom; sometimes a process in which a relief plate
is made by etching away parts of the zinc; especially a process,
the same in principle as lithography, in which a zinc plate re-
places stone.

### zincography, process of

A negative photographic plate of the original matter is taken.
It is then transferred to the zinc plate, by exposure to light.
After inking, cleaning, dusting with powdered resin, heating,
and coating with acid, the "zinc print" is mounted type high
and prints are made from it.

# PART II

# Names in the History of Writing, Printing, Publishing, Book Collecting, Book Selling, and Library Development

# A

Achard
>In 1806-1807 he wrote at Marseilles the earliest textbook for the study of bibliography, Cours Elementaire de Bibliographie.

Ackermann, Rudolph (1764-1834)
>A German designer and director of art activities, he was one of the earliest popularizes of lithography. In 1808 he began his great series of illustrated books with Microcosm of London, using Rowlandson, an eminent English caricaturist, as illustrator.

Acton, Lord
>In 1902 his valuable library of 60,000 volumes was presented to the Cambridge University Library.

Aitken, Robert (1734-1802)
>In 1782 he brought out at Philadelphia the first English Bible to be printed in America.

Albertsen, Dr. Peter
>His books of canon law and medicine represent the foundation volumes for the University of Copenhagen Library (15th century).

Aldus
A native Italian named Aldo Manuzio, but better known as Aldus, he was the founder of the family and the press which bears his name, and the inventor of the dolphin and anchor device which marks an "Aldine." In 1501 he began to print the long series of pocket classics for which he is best known, for which series, in the same year, he brought out the first italic type (made by Griffi) in editions of Virgil and Juvenal. The idea for the italic is supposed to have come to him after he saw the slanting handwriting in a manuscript of Francis Petrarch.

Allacci, Leone
The alphabetical index of Greek manuscripts which he compiled for the Vatican Library in 1620 is still in use.

Amerbach, Hans (1444-1513)
In 1494 at Basle, he printed the first great reference work on medieval authors De Scriptoribus Ecclesiasticis, a catalogue by the pioneer bibliographer Tritheim.

Amman, Jost
One of the few eminent German designers of the later sixteenth century. He made outstanding illustrations for Theatrum Mulienum (1586), and his Panoplia Omnium Artium (1574) contained excellent woodcut pictures of the various craftsmen of the time, including the best known early picture of a woodcutter at work.

Amstel, J. C. Ploos van
An amateur engraver of Amsterdam (1726-1798), who may have produced aquatints before Le Prince, the man generally believed to have invented aquatint. Amstel's plates often combined aquatint with etched lines and with roulette work.

Anderson, Edwin Hatfield
First librarian of the Carnegie Library at Pittsburgh, state librarian of New York at Albany, he was appointed director of the New York Public Library on May 14, 1913 and guided the institution through the troublous years of the great war and the uncertain period that followed.

Andreani, Andrea
In medieval times, one of the leading Italian exponents of

chiaroscuro. His work, like that of his contemporaries in Italy, France, Germany, and other countries, consisted mainly of individual plates, rather than of book illustrations.

Applegarth, Augustus
A nineteenth-century inventor and engineer. In 1827 he and Edward Cowper jointly invented a four-cylinder printing machine; in 1848, Applegarth, for the London Times, con- structed the first rotary press. The distinctive features of this machine were: the ability to print both sides of the sheet at the same time; the impressive inking apparatus; the ex- ceptional speed, the new machine being capable of printing 50,000 copies an hour.

Arethas (860-940)
Archbishop of Caesarea (an ancient seaport in northwest Israel), the Roman capital of Palestine, he possessed the largest private library of the time (900 A.D.).

Arrighi, Ludovico
A member of the Papal chancery, in 1524 he cut a notably original italic type, preserving closely the effect of manuscript. From him and Aldus descend all italic fonts.

Ashbee, Charles Robert (1863-1942)
In 1898, he and Coomaraswamy founded the Essex House Press, London.

Augustus, Gaius Julius Caesar Octavianus (63 B.C.-A.D.14)
A title of honor and sacred majesty, first conferred upon Octavianus Caesar as head of the Roman priesthood, and later used commonly by Roman emperors; also, Augustus, political heir to Caesar and executor of so many of his projects, who founded the Octavian Library in the Porticus Octaviae in 33 B.C. and the Bibliotheca Palatina in 28 B.C.

# B

**Badier, Florimonde**
The possible identity of the French binder called Le Gascon, developer and modifier, in the seventeenth century, of the binding style known as fanfare.

**Badius, Jocius**
A scholar-printer whose press quickly won renown for clarity and thoroughness of its texts and the quality of its printing. He is also remembered for his device, which first appeared in his edition of Priscian's Institutiones Grammaticae (1507), the first representation of a press in action.

**Ballantyne, James**
Part owner of the printing firm of James Ballantyne & Co. A secret partner in the firm for a time was Sir Walter Scott.

**Bologna, Francesco da**
Petrarch's beautiful script is said to have been the basis for the semicursive type (the Aldine), which he cut for the Aeneid, printed by Aldus Manutius at Venice in 1501.

**Barker, Christopher**
A very successful printer-publisher of the sixteenth century. He was appointed royal printer to Elizabeth and was succeeded, upon his death, by his son Robert Barker.

**Barth, J. A.**
One of the earliest experimenters in color lithography.

**Bartholomaeus, Anglicus**
His De Proprietatibus Rerum, published in 1495-1496, is the first printed on English paper.

**Baskerville, John**
An outstanding English printer of the eighteenth century. In the preface to his edition of Paradise Lost, he observed that his aim was to print, not many books, but only those which were works of consequence, intrinsic merit, or accepted reputation.

He established his own foundry in 1750-1752 and proceeded to carefully design types and to cut them with extraordinary skill. He even constructed his own printing press (starting about 1752). He is generally given credit for the invention of the metal-based move mold and for being the first to use wove paper in his edition of Virgil, printed in 1757.

Baskett, John
An important printer of the eighteenth century, known best for his famous edition of the Bible, printed in 1716-1717, frequently referred to, by virtue of its misprints, as the <u>Vinegar</u> <u>Bible</u>. The work was impressively printed in a large roman font and matching italic.

Bateman, John and Abraham
King's printers and binders. It is believed generally that many of the most pleasing (and often most elaborate) bindings of the early seventeenth century were done by them.

Baxter, George
A nineteenth-century draughtsman, colorist, and painstaking printer, equally skilled in line engraving, aquatinting, and mezzotinting. In 1835 he took out a patent for a new process of color illustration, his method being to print the outline and detail of his design and then to add color by means of successive impressions from separate blocks of wood or metal. His finest color plates are doubtless those which appeared in his <u>Pictorial</u> <u>Album</u>, issued by Chapman and Hall in 1836.

Becket, Isaac
The first professional mezzotinter in England and a very successful seventeenth-century reproducer of portraits.

Beckford, William (1759-1840)
A noted British collector of books, particularly those books which were singular or impressive for their illustrations and fine printing.

Bellaert, Jacob
He began printing in 1483 and is the first known printer in Haarlem, Holland.

**Bembo, Pietro**
    A letter written in 1501 states that it was Bembo who secured
    the actual manuscript which Petrarch had written with his own
    hand, each letter of which was precisely copied by Aldus Manutius
    and reproduced in his italic faces.

**Bensley, Thomas**
    An English printer of the late eighteenth century, he devoted a
    great deal of his time to the production of finely printed editions.
    Among his best works were an edition of Thomson's The Seasons
    (1787), the Bible in seven volumes (1800), and Hume's History
    of England (1806).

**Berchtold**
    His use in 1855 of Talbot's screen principle to effect graduated
    tones, rather than shadows only, marked the beginning of half-
    tone photo etching in England. The invention reached relative
    perfection in 1880 in the hands of Meisenbach in England, Petit
    in France, Horgan and Ives in America.

**Berkeley, Bishop**
    His gift in 1733 to the Yale University Library of one thousand
    choice volumes is claimed to be greater than any which pre-
    ceded or followed it for nearly a hundred years, one of the
    finest which, as a collection, was ever brought to America.

**Berners, Juliana, The Bokys of Hauking and Hunting**
    The first printed English book in which colored inks were used
    for illustration; the first book on field sports; first English
    book on heraldry; first English book containing English popular
    rhymes.

**Berthelet, Thomas**
    Royal Printer and, for a time, Royal Binder to Henry VIII,
    outstanding both for good workmanship and good taste. Among
    his impressive works were: Sir Thomas Elyot's Boke Named
    the Governour, an octavo printed in fine Gothic type; a folio
    edition of Gower's Confessio Amantis (1532); an edition (in
    1533) of Erasmus' De Immensa Misericordia.

**Bessarion, Cardinal**
    In his attempt to build up the largest Greek library in the world,
    he sent agents to all parts of Greece and Asia Minor in search

174

of manuscripts. Most of his works eventually went to the Biblioteca Marciana in Venice.

Bettini, Antonio (1396-1487)
His Monte Sancto di Dio, printed at Florence by Niccolo di Lorenzo, 1477, contains the first known copper engraved illustrations printed directly on text-page and, possibly, the first use of intaglio illustration in a printed book.

Bewick, Thomas
Born in England in 1753, he is the first master of the modern method of white-line wood engraving, done with a burin on end grain. His technique revolutionized the art and exerted strong influence on book design and typefaces.

Beza, Theodore
In 1581 he presented to the Cambridge University Library the famous Codex of the Gospels, which has ever since borne his name. The Bezae is the earliest two-language manuscript, the left-hand page being in Greek, the right-hand page being in Latin.

Bill, John
King's Printer to James I, he issued in 1617 the first London edition of the Frankfurt Mess Katalog, which he thereafter published twice yearly until 1628. At first these editions were merely replicas of the German lists, but in 1622, John Bill issued the first to contain an English supplement.

Billings, John Shaw
A surgeon of the United States Army, he was the virtual creator of the Army Medical Library (the largest medical library in the world), a very important participant in the planning of the Johns Hopkins Hospital, and a one-time director of the New York Public Library.

Billingsley
His Pen's Excellency or Secretary's Delight, published in 1618, was the first of a large series of copybooks of "copperplate" writing in England.

Biscop, Benedict
He founded a monastery at Wearmouth in the seventh century

and endowed it with a small library; later, he founded a second
library at Jarrow.

Bishop, Dr. William Warner
Sent by the Carnegie Corporation in 1926 to survey the Vatican
Library and made recommendations for its future growth and
development.

Blackwood, William
A nineteenth-century English bookseller and publisher. In 1816
he secured publishing rights to the first series of Scott's <u>Tales
of My Landlord,</u> and in 1817 he began the publication of the
<u>Edinburgh Monthly Magazine</u>. He later acquired shares in the
works of Byron and Shelley.

Blades, William (1824-1890)
A great bibliographer, he died in 1890. The following year,
his collection became the nucleus of the St. Bride Typographical
Library of London.

Blaeu, Willem Janszoon (1571-1638)
A founder of the printing family at Amsterdam and a carto-
grapher of lasting fame, he introduced an important improvement in the printing press in 1620; namely, the platen spring,
which cut the work of the pressman by half.

Blake, William
An eighteenth-century poet and a very imaginative employer
of wood engraving.

Blooteling, Abraham
A seventeenth-century Dutch engraver who greatly advanced
the technique of mezzotint, a process apparently invented by
Von Siegen at Amsterdam. He lived in England from 1673 to
1676. While he may not have invented the mezzotint rocker
(a tool used to obtain a desirable ground on the plate), he was
probably the first to systematically and effectively use the
rocker, as well as the scraper and burnisher.

Blotius, Hugo
First one to catalogue the collections of the Austrian National
Library and to secure for it the legal deposit law.

Bodine, Giambattista
An outstanding Italian printer of the eighteenth century.

Bodley, Sir Thomas
The founder of the Bodleian Library (the Oxford University
Library). Before his death in 1613, he had the satisfaction of
witnessing the three events of 1610 which more than secured
the future growth of the Bodleian: the confirmation of the Code
of Statutes for its government; the agreement with the Stationers'
Company by which the Bodleian was to receive a perfect copy of
every book printed in the Stationers' Company; the beginning
of the expansion of the library buildings.

Bodoni, Francesco
Italian printer, and father of a more famous printer, Giambattista Bodoni.

Bodoni, Giambattista
One of the great names in Italian printing and an engraver of
some consequence. His first edition of his Manuale Tipographico,
published in 1788, contained 150 Latin and 28 Greek characters
of his own engraving; his second edition, published posthumously,
contained 291 complete alphabets, including Greek and Oriental
letters. Among his outstanding printed works are: Epithalamia
(1775), printed in twenty-five languages and decorated with copper engravings by leading artists of the day; Anacreon (1784),
and Tasso's Aminta (1789).

Bogue
In 1845 he originated inexpensive reprints of standard works,
a method of publication later turned into a very successful
enterprise by H. G. Bohn.

Bomberg, Daniel (fl. 1516-1549)
In 1520 he printed at Venice the first complete edition of the
Babylonian Talmud, the pagination of which is adhered to for
following centuries.

Bonnet, Louis (1735-1793)
By printing a crayon engraving in various colors, using a
separate plate for each tone, he approximated the quality of
pastel. So far as is known, he was the first to effect this.

Bönner, Caspar
The founder and first librarian of the Leipzig University Library,
to which he left as the foundation collection his own library, rich
in early printed books. Before his death in 1547 he compiled a
catalogue of the manuscripts which was published in 1608 (<u>Cata-
logus</u> <u>codicum</u> <u>manuscriptorum</u> <u>bibliothecae</u> <u>Paulinae</u>).

Borromeo, Cardinal Frederic (1564-1631)
He founded the Ambrosiana Library in 1608 and donated to it the
foundation collection, the literary treasures collected by him
with great care and at extraordinary expense. The opening collection consisted of 12,000 manuscripts and 30,000 printed
works, to be used, not only by the ecclesiastics, but by the
public; not the citizens of Milan only, but by anyone from any
nation.

Bowyer, William
An English eighteenth-century printer who rendered invaluable
service to English typography by his support of Caslon, a support which enabled Caslon to establish a typefoundry in which
he produced types superior to those which had up to then been
imported from Holland.

Boyet
He is credited with perfecting the Jansenist style of binding
and with being the first to use the dentelle pattern on doublure.
He was binder to the King of France in 1698.

Bradford, William
He has the distinction of having introduced printing to both
Philadelphia and New York. He set up a press in Philadelphia
in 1685 and in 1693 was made Royal Printer at New York.

Bradshaw, Henry
Celebrated librarian of the Cambridge University Library,
around whose influence and work most of the progress of the
library during the second half of the nineteenth century centered. Between 1867 and 1886 he gave to the library his collections of Irish and liturgical books and added nearly a hundred volumes to the "Early Printed Books."

Braille, Louis (1809-1852)
In 1829 he published at Paris the rudiments of his system of writing
for the blind.

Bray, Thomas (1656-1730)
His establishment in South Carolina (in 1700) of the first of his thirty-nine parochial libraries marked the beginning of the popular library movement in North America.

Breitkopf, Johann Gottlob Immanuel (1719-1794)
The most productive German typefounder of the eighteenth century, he was the first to set some of Goethe's poems to music. After ten years of experimentation, he evolved in 1754 a new method of rendering musical notations in type, the basis of music printing today.

Breydenbach, Bernard (1482-1498)
His Peregrinationes in Terram Sanctam, printed and illustrated by Reuwich at Mainz in 1486, is the first book with folded impressions from woodcuts, and the earliest known example of a painter of distinction illustrating a printed book.

Brocar
During 1514-1518 he printed, at Alcalá de Henares, the first great polyglot Bible, known as the Complutensian. A monument of Spanish typography, it is regarded as one of the world's most splendid books, containing the first Hebrew Bible published by Christians and the first separately printed Greek New Testament.

Brown, John Carter (1797-1874)
One of America's best known book collectors, his entire library was given to Brown University in 1900, a library especially rich in early Americana, travels and explorations. Today it is considered one of the finest collections of Americana in existence.

Brown, William
He and Thomas Gilmore introduced printing into Quebec in 1764, their first venture being the Quebec Gazette, printed in English and French.

Brunet, Jacques Charles (1780-1867)
His Manuel de l'ameteur des Livres is a great French bibliographic work, perhaps the only comprehensive bibliography, based on Parisian antiquarian book lore, which is still useful today.

**Buckingham, Duke of**

His gift to the Cambridge University Library of the Oriental MSS. from the library of Thomas Erpenius, the distinguished linguist, was one of the most important in the seventeenth century.

**Bullen, A.H.**

In 1904 he founded the Shakespeare Head Press at Stratford, to print the poet's works in his native town, using only Stratford men. The Stratford Town Shakespeare in ten volumes was completed in 1907.

**Bullen, H. L.**

In 1908 he established at Jersey City the Typographical Library of American Type Founders Company.

**Bulmer, William**

An outstanding English printer of the eighteenth century, he became the printer to the Shakespeare Press in 1787, a press founded primarily to publish an edition of Shakespeare's works illustrated from the drawings in John Boydell's Pall Mall Gallery. The work, known as Boydell's Shakespeare was issued in nine volumes between 1791 and 1805.

**Bure, Guillaume François de (1731-1782)**

A renowned French book collector, his Bibliographie Instructive, published during the later half of the eighteenth century, is the first general bibliophilic list. In this work, too, the term bibliography is first used in the modern sense of writing about books.

**Burgess, Hugh**

In 1851 he and Charles Watt successfully produced a form of chemical wood pulp suitable for papermaking. They patented their process in America in 1854.

**Burne-Jones, Sir Edward Coley (1833-1898)**

One of the leading artists of the Victorian era, whose designs were translated onto wood for engraved book illustrations.

**Burney, Charles**

His library of some 13,000 volumes and 500 early Greek and Latin manuscripts was acquired by the British Museum in 1817. Also important in the Burney library were files of seventeenth-

and eighteenth-century British newspapers, bound chronologically and indexed by Burney himself.

Burton, Robert
A bequest made by him in 1640 permitted the Bodleian Library
to take from his library any books which it lacked. As a result,
the Bodleian is indebted to Burton for some of its rarest and
most curious works, among them one of the only two known
copies of the edition of Venus and Adonis of 1602.

Bylaert, Jacob
Said to have invented the process of stipple engraving in 1760.

# C

Callimachus (also Callemachus)
Chief librarian at the great library of Alexandria. Of about 800
works ascribed to him, only a few are extant.

Callot, Jacques (1594-1635)
In 1630 he substituted aqua fortis for the burin in making copperplates. Doing so marked the beginning of a lighter and more
graceful style of illustration.

Camusat, Jean (?-1639)
The first printer of the French Academy, founded in 1635 by
Cardinal Richelieu.

Capen, Edward
The first librarian of the Boston Public Library.

Capodistrias, John
In 1828 he founded the National Library of Greece which, until
1832, remained an integral part of the newly founded National
Museum.

Carlegle

His illustrations for <u>Daphnis</u> et <u>Chloe</u>, in 1919, marked the beginning of an innovation in wood engraving, the use of burin to approximate the effects of brush strokes.

Carlyle, Alexander

The nephew of Thomas Carlyle, in 1929 and 1930 he presented papers of the famous nineteenth-century author to the Edinburgh, The National Library of Scotland.

Carnegie, Andrew

Beginning in 1881 he encouraged the construction of free public libraries with his gift of a library to the Pittsburgh town in which his steelworkers lived. By 1920 he had provided assistance toward the construction of some 2,500 library buildings in the United States.

Carpi, Ugo da

It has been claimed that he was the first to practice the form of color printing known as chiaroscuro. In any event he is known to have applied in 1516 to the Venetian Senate for a copyright to protect his chiaroscuro process.

Casanate, Girolamo

A cardinal and once librarian at the Vatican Library, he donated 160,000 <u>scudi</u> and his personal library of 50,000 volumes to found a library for public use in the Dominican monastery of the Minerva, the Biblioteca Casanatense. In 1925 the library possessed 130,000 printed volumes, 85,000 pamphlets, and 2,080 incunabula; 6,000 manuscripts, among them 64 Greek manuscripts and 230 Hebrew texts.

Caslon, William

An eighteenth-century English engraver of gun stocks and barrels, he changed to type cutting and in 1720 opened a foundry. His success was almost immediate, his roman and italic being accepted as superior to the others and purchased even by foreign printers.

Cassiodorus, Flavius Magnus Aurelius (c.485-c.580)

In 539 he organized the literary work of the scriptorium at Calabria, making it a model for the book preserving monasteries of Europe.

Castaldi, Pamfilo
> While not the inventor of movable types, as some have claimed, he was the first printer in Milan, Italy.

Cawood, John
> An English printer of the sixteenth century. He was master of the Stationers' Company and succeeded Grafton as Royal Printer upon the accession of Queen Mary. He is best known for his many editions of the Book of Common Prayer and for his edition of Barclay's translation of the Ship of Fools.

Caxton, William (c.1422-1491)
> He was the first English printer, his first printed book being his own translation of the Receuil, with the English title The Recuyell of the Historyes of Troye. Although undated, unsigned, and unplaced, it is generally believed to have been printed at Bruges between 1472 and 1474. The first dated book printed by Caxton, issued on November 18, 1477, was the Dictes and Sayengis of the Philosophres. In all, between 1476 and his death in 1491, Caxton printed about one-hundred books, the most notable being: Chaucer's Canterbury Tales (1478), Gower's Confession Amantis (1485), and Malory's Morte D'Arthur (1485).

Cenaculo, Manuel do
> His gift of books and manuscripts were part of the foundation collections of the Lisbon: A Biblioteca Nacional (the national library of Lisbon).

Cennini
> He was the first to establish a press at Florence (1471) and, in making type for his magnificent Commentario di Servio su Virgilio, may have been the first Italian typefounder.

Champollion, Jean François (1790-1832)
> Decipherer of the Rosetta Stone and founder of modern Egyptology.

Charles I
> Founded the National Library of Czechoslovakia in 1348.

Charles III
> Founded the Royal Library of Naples in 1734 which, in 1804, was opened to the public. Perhaps the most remarkable possession of the library is a collection of papyri from Herculaneum.

**Charles V**

His library, established in the Louvre, was one of the libraries which were incorporated into the Bibliotheque Nationale de France, the oldest of European national libraries.

**Charless, Joseph**

He introduced printing in St. Louis when, in 1808, he founded the Missouri Gazette at the old French settlement of Saint Louis.

**Chasanowitz, Dr. Joseph**

He founded the Jewish National and University Library when, in 1895, he sent the first consignment of some 8,800 books to Jerusalem.

**Chepman, Walter**

In 1507 he and Andrew Myllar printed the first books in Scotland. These survive in one copy in the National Library of Scotland.

**Chew, Beverly**

A part of her library, a collection particularly rich in the poetry of the seventeenth century and numbering about 1,600 volumes, was acquired by the Huntington Library in 1912.

**Church, Elihu Dwight**

His library, especially strong in Americana and in the early editions of such English poets as Shakespeare, Spenser, and Milton, numbering 2,133 volumes, was acquired by Mr. Huntington in 1911 (his first really extensive acquisition).

**Chrysostom, St. John (c.347-407) (also Chrysostomus)**

His Homilae, as printed by Lauer at Rome in 1470, is the first work in which page numbers are used (arabic numerals at the top).

**Clement V, Pope**

The publication of Pope Clement V's Constitutiones in 1460 by Fust and Schoeffer is held to be the first printed law book.

**Clymer, George**

With the construction of The Columbian Press, as he called it, in 1816, he dispensed with the screw, depending entirely upon levers.

Cobden-Sanderson, Thomas James (1840-1922)
   An impressive and influential binder, his work in the 1880's
   had much to do with the resurrection of leather bindings.

Cobham, Thomas de
   Established the first official Oxford University Library in 1410,
   at which time it was called Cobham's Library and enjoyed the
   patronage of Henry IV. It was housed in the upper floor of the
   Old Congregation House on the north side of St. Mary's Chancel.

Colbert, Jean Baptiste (1619-1683)
   He secured for the Bibliotheque Nationale de France, under the
   reign of Louis XIV, many of its finest pieces. In 1663 he founded
   the Academy of Inscriptions.

Cole, George Watson
   The first librarian of the Huntington Library, and the first to
   attempt to catalogue the collection of rare books.

Colines, Simon de
   A French printer and scholar of the sixteenth century. He
   introduced into France the use of 16mo editions; he contributed
   to the replacement of Gothic type forms by roman; he was the
   first French printer to set a book entirely in italic.

Comenius, John Amos (1592-1670)
   His production in 1657 of Orbis Sensualium Pictus (World Illustrated) is the first illustrated school book for children.

Congreve, Sir William
   In 1818 he invented the colored watermarking of paper, and
   during the two following years he took out patents to protect
   his process of multicolor printing from metal plates.

Constable, Archibald
   A bookseller and publisher, he first gained fame by his publication in 1802 of the first numbers of the Edinburgh Review. He
   also published among other works Scott's Lay of the Last Minstrel
   and the poem Marmion. In 1814 he bought the copyright of the Encyclopedia Britannica from Adam and Charles Black.

Conwell
   In 1900 he established the Elston Press at New Rochelle, New

York, the first attempt in America to revive the handpress method.

Coolidge, Archibald Cary
The first director and one of the most generous benefactors of the Harvard University Library.

Copinger, Walter A.
His work Supplement (1895-1902) represented an important contribution to the beginning of the modern bibliography of incunabula.

Corvinus, Matthias
King of Hungary from 1458 to 1490, he was a noteworthy collector of the finest manuscript books, preferring them to volumes produced by printing. He had his scribes write manuscript books, commissioned miniature painters to illuminate them, and secured binders to design handsome covers for them.

Cosimo
Opened the Medici Library in 1444.

Coster, Laurens Janszoon
It is claimed by some that he printed in 1448 the popular Latin grammar De Octo Partibus Orationis by Donatus, perhaps the first book in Europe printed from movable types; also that he printed the Abecedarium, a work which may have been printed as early as 1440.

Cotton, Sir Robert
Took up the work in 1572, begun by Archbishop Parker, of gathering and preserving the records of English literature and history (including coins as well as MSS.), which had been dispersed by the dissolution of the monasteries half a century before. Such was his success that his library, one of the foundations of the British Museum Library, has been described as possibly the most splendid of all those in the Department of Manuscripts, although numbering only about a thousand volumes. Included are the unique copy of Beowulf, Sir Gawain and the Green Knight, and the C text of Piers Plowman.

Coverdale, Miles (1488-1568)
His second English Bible, printed in 4to and folio by Nycolson at Southwark in 1537, is the first complete English Bible ever printed in England.

Cowley, Sir A. E.
   Librarian of the Bodleian Library from 1919 to 1931 who produced the extraordinary <u>Concise Catalogue of the Hebrew Books</u>.
   It was he also who was largely responsible for the appointment
   of the Commission to inquire into the library provision in Oxford and for recommendàtions which his successor, Dr. H. H. E.
   Craster, carried out.

Cowper, Edward
   A nineteenth-century printer and inventor who, in 1818,
   patented several improvements in printing, including a better
   system of ink distribution and a better plan for conveying sheets
   from the cylinders of the press.

Cracherode, Rev. Clayton Mordaunt
   An outstanding eighteenth-century book collector who in 1784
   became a Trustee of the British Museum and upon his death in
   1799, bequeathed to it his collection of 4,500 volumes, mostly
   in classical literature, <u>belles lettres</u>, and works of divinity,
   but including many incunabula of first quality, not to mention a
   large and valuable collection of gems and prints. The collection
   was also distinguished by the extraordinary condition of the
   volumes, many of the bindings being specially executed for Rev.
   Cracherode by Roger Payne.

Cramoisy, Sebastien
   He was the first director of the Imprimerie Royale, founded
   in 1640 by Louis XIV. The leading Parisian printer of the time,
   his first production as director of the Imprimerie Royale du
   Louvre was <u>De Imitatione Christi,</u> with copperplate illustrations
   by Poussin.

Cranz, Martin
   One of three Germans who set up the press at the Sorbonne in
   1470 which marked the beginning of printing in France.

Cromwell, Oliver
   In 1654 he presented to the Bodleian Library twenty Greek
   manuscripts and two Russian manuscripts, part of the Barocci
   Collection which had not yet been acquired by the Bodleian.

Cruikshank, George (1792-1818)
He was one of several artists in England who were the first to develop the art of line etching for book illustration. Cruikshank's influence dominated England for much of the nineteenth century.

Cumont, Franz Valéry Marie (1868-1947)
In 1923 he unearthed on the site of the Roman fortress of Dura, in the Upper Euphrates, vellum documents which antedate the two found in Jurdistan in 1909.

Curil, Edmund
Notorious for his simultaneous publications of religious works and obscene works and, to an even greater extent, for his quarrels with Alexander Pope.

Cusi, Meschullam
He was the first printer to use Hebrew type.

Cutter, Charles Ammi
The first librarian at the Newberry Library in Chicago, he devised a classification system, named after him, to compete with his chief rival Dewey. A later and more complicated system was formulated by him named the "Expansive Classification."

# D

Daguerre, Louis Jacques Mandé (1787-1851)
In 1839 the French government first published his photographic process, known as daguerreotype.

Daniel, Charles H. Clive (1836-1919)
In 1876, while Provost of the University of Oxford, he uncovered the Fell types after 150 years of disuse, with eleven productions at Frome, and fifty-nine productions at Oxford.

**Danner**
A Nuremberg printer who, in 1550, improved the printing press with a tympan, frisket, and a metal screw in place of the wooden one--the first mechanical improvements in a century.

**Daumier, Honoré (1808-1879)**
From 1833 to 1870 he designed woodcut illustrations which were equalled only by those designed during the period of 1470-1520.

**Davis, James**
In 1749 he set up his press at New Bern, North Carolina, in response to the government's urgent need of someone to print its laws, which marked the introduction of printing in North Carolina.

**Davison, Thomas**
An important printer of the nineteenth century. He printed most of Byron's works and many of those of Campbell, Moore, and Wordsworth.

**Day, John (1522-1584)**
Perhaps the best and most enterprising printer of his time, the introducer of fine types and initials, and the first English type-founder to cut roman and italic letters to the same size, so that they could be used together most advantageously. Among his notable publications were: Foxe's Book of Martyrs, 2,008 folio pages, printed in double columns in a small Black Letter type; Norton's Tragedy of Gorboduc (1570); and Ascham's Scholemaster (1570). His publication of Parker's De Antiquitate Britannicae Ecclesiae in 1572 was the first privately printed book brought out in England.

**Day, Matthew**
The son of Stephen Day, he took over in 1647 control of the press founded by his father.

**Day, Stephen**
He introduced printing in America by establishing a press in 1638 at Cambridge, Massachusetts. The first book published by Day's press, of which copies are still extent, was The Whole Booke of Psalmes Faithfully Translated into English Metre, now better known as the Bay Psalm Book, published in 1640.

About 1,700 copies of this work were printed, but only eleven of these are known to be still extant, and of these only four are perfect.

de Bry, Thomas
He was the illustrator of the most famous sixteenth-century book with copperplate engravings, the Collectiones Peregrinatiorum in Indiam, Orientalem, et Occidentalem.

Debucourt, Louis Philibert
Probably best known for his brilliant pictures of Parisian habits and dress before and during the French Revolution. Among his finest pieces were: Promenade de la Galerie de Palais Royale (1787) and Promenade Publique (1792).

Debure, Guillaume François (1731-1782)
Author of Bibliographie Instructive, the first significant bibliography, published at Paris in 1763.

De Gregomiis, Gregorius and John
In 1492 they published an edition of Boccaccio's Decameron, notable for an opening page which contained a large illustrative woodcut over seventeen lines of text, with the whole surrounded by an elaborate architectural border.

Delisle, Leopold (1874-1907)
A medievalist who, although mainly interested in manuscripts and paleographical studies, did much to modernize the Bibliotheque Nationale and to make it available to scholars from all over the world.

Demarteau, Gilles (1756-1802)
Jean Charles François is generally credited with being the inventor of the crayon method (which aims to render the effect of chalk drawing), but Demarteau excelled François in both quality and quantity of output.

Derome, Nicholas Denis
One of the most important French binders of the eighteenth century and an expert in the dentelle style. He introduced an original tool, a small bird with outstretched wings, which he used in his designs with notable effect.

De Vinne, Theodore
    A student of the history of printing and an author of numerous
    books on the typography of the past, he made significant con-
    tributions in the field of illustrations. A notable American
    printer of the twentieth century.

Dewey, Melvil
    In 1876, while he was the librarian of Amherst College, Mass-
    achusetts, he developed his system of decimals for classifying
    knowledge, as he went about his task of recataloging the library.
    All knowledge, according to the system, is divided into ten classes
    from 0 to 9, each class into a maximum of ten divisions, and
    each division into a maximum of ten sections (each of the sub-
    division types being also divided from 0 to 9). The broad divi-
    sions are: 0 General works; 1 Philosophy; 2 Religion; 3 Political
    economy and law ("Social sciences"); 4 Philology; 5 Pure sciences
    and mathematics; 6 Applied sciences and useful arts; 7 Fine arts;
    8 Literature; 9 History and geography.

de Worde, Wynkyn
    He succeeded Caxton to the press in 1491 upon his death. His
    first works were printed with Caxton's types, but Liber Festi-
    valis (1493) was printed with his own type and was the first book
    to bear his name as printer. Three of the books which he
    printed in 1495 are of particular interest: Vitas Patrum, a work
    which Caxton had finished translating on the very day of his
    death; De Proprietatibus Rerum, famous for its epilogue in
    which de Worde wrote of Caxton and identified the paper on
    which the matter was printed as having come from the mill of
    John Tate, England's earliest known paper maker; Polychronicon,
    a reprint of Higden's work and the first English book to contain
    printed music. De Worde's printing of Wakefield's Oratio marked
    the first English attempt to cut Arabic and Hebrew letters.

Diarmid, King
    In 567 he sat in judgment at Tara, Ireland on what was probably
    the first copyright case in Europe. The main litigant was St.
    Columba, who appeared in defense of his transcript of an abbot's
    psalter.

Dickinmutt, Conrad
    A fifteenth-century printer known for his fine illustrations.
    One of his outstanding works was an edition of the Eunuchus
    of Terence (1486).

Dickinson, John

In 1809 he perfected and patented his cylinder papermaking machine. He also invented a machine for making cardboard, and a method of producing paper with silken or cotton thread running through it.

Didot, François (1689-1759)

A bookseller and printer, founder of the family of printers who made their name the outstanding one in eighteenth-century French printing. His most impressive work was a twenty-one volume edition of the works of Abbé Prevost, illustrated with maps and engravings.

François Ambroise Didot (1720-1804)   The elder son of François Didot. He invented a form of hand press; he designed several new roman and italic types; he fixed the point at approximately 1/72 of an inch; he introduced a hot dressed paper much like that used by Baskerville in England; he instructed Benjamin Franklin's grandson (Benjamin Franklin Bache) in the mysteries of type-founding.

Firmin Didot   Younger son of François Ambroise Didot, he is noteworthy for several reasons: he made various improvements in the type designs which his father created; he received many awards for his printing excellence; he was the first person to make use of stereotype for book printing.

Pierre Didot (1764-1853)   The elder son of François Ambroise Didot, he too was an outstanding printer and publisher. One of his outstanding works was an edition of the works of Racine which, exhibited in 1801, was awarded a prize as the finest book ever printed, "the finest typographical achievement of all ages."

Pierre François Didot (1732-1793)   The younger son of François Didot, brother of François Ambroise Didot. Appointed printer to the Dauphin in 1759, he produced several exceptional works; but he is better known as the founder of a paper mill at Essonnes, which became in time the most important one in France. He had two sons who contributed to the history of printing and book production: Henri Didot (1765-1852), who produced a microscopic type of unusual interest; St. Leger Didot (1767-1829), who was the first person to produce paper in an endless roll, an innovation which contributed to the growth of the newspaper press.

Digby, Sir Kenelm
In 1634 he gave to the Bodleian Library his collection of two hundred and thirty-eight manuscripts, dealing with the early history of science in England and with the general history of England.

Dockway, Thomas
He was the first master of the Company of Stationers (sixteenth century).

Dodsley, Robert
Notable for his association with Dr. Samuel Johnson, whose London: A Poem he printed. It was Dodsley who suggested to Johnson that he work on the Dictionary that the latter completed in 1755 and it was Dodsley who published The Rambler, a bi-weekly periodical which appeared regularly for two years and was entirely written by Dr. Johnson.

Dokyo
A Buddhist monk and later chief physician to the Japanese Empress who probably introduced papermaking into Japan; for it was soon after his arrival in Japan that paper, made from the bark of the mulberry tree, was manufactured there about 610 A.D.

Donaldson, Alexander
An Edinburgh bookseller and publisher who in 1775 challenged the perpetual copyright which was held to exist in common law by submitting an appeal to the House of Lords. The House of Lords reversed the decision of the lower court, which had gone against Donaldson, relative to his reprinting of Thomson's The Seasons, and decided that no permanent copyright existed in common law.

Doni
His Libraria, the first Italian national bibliography, was published at Venice during the years 1550-1560.

**Donkin**

He and Bacon constructed the first rotary press in 1813. It was Bryan Donkin, a printing engineer, who discovered the method of casting a cylinder on metal stock, of treacle and glue melted together, and, by this means, of solving the problem of inking.

**Doré, Paul Gustave (1833-1883)**

He was the most popular of the representative nineteenth-century illustrators on the Continent. In 1848 he began his work on Journal pour Rire.

**D'Orville, James Philip**

A distinguished classical scholar, whose collection of manuscripts, 1,750 volumes of mainly Greek and Latin classics, was acquired in 1805 by the Bodleian Library.

**Douce, Francis**

In 1830 he bequeathed The Douce Collection to the Bodleian Library, composed of 393 manuscripts, 98 charters, 17,000 printed volumes, and a large group of early and valuable prints and drawings. The Douce Collection is exceptionally rich in Bibles, Horae, Primers, Books of Common Prayer, and Psalters.

**Draeger**

In 1887 he founded at Paris a printing house which later played an important role in the reform of French printing.

**Du Pre, Jean**

In 1481 he issued at Paris the first book with woodcut illustrations, Paris Missal, a work which contained a single and somewhat crudely designed picture of the Crucifixion.

**Dürer, Albrecht**

An outstanding woodcut designer of the fifteenth century, a master in the craft of creating halftones by means of cross-hatching, and a profound influence on his successors. In 1498 he began his important work with a series of sixteen woodcuts of the Apocalypse, published in book form at Nuremberg. In 1516 he engraved the first dated bookplate known.

# E

**Eadfrith or Eadfrid (d. 721)**
In 635 A.D. he made a copy of the Gospels, now known as the
"Durham Book" and preserved in the British Museum, which is
accounted the best example of Anglo-Saxon round-hand of the
time.

**Eberhard**
In 1805 he experimented at Magdeburg with zinc as an etching
medium for relief printing, and, so doing, began a movement
toward the use of zinc for surface printing in place of stone.

**Ebert, Friedrich Adolph (1791-1834)**
Acclaimed the greatest German bibliographer, his definition of
bibliography as "the science of books" did much to advance the
concept. Author of Allgemeines Bibliographisches Lexikon.

**Edwards, James**
An eighteenth-century English binder, he discovered the method
of ornamenting bindings in calf by impressing them with ordinary
stamps treated with acid. His bindings are generally called
Etruscan because of their classical designs.

**Egenolf-Berner**
In 1592 the first typefounder's specimen sheet was published
by the Egenolf-Berner foundry at Frankfurt-am-Main.

**Eggestein, Heinrich**
A very important fifteenth-century printer at Strassburg.
Among his important works were three Bibles printed in Latin
and a hugh folio edition of Decretum Gratiana. In 1466 he issued the earliest known printed book advertisement (fifteen
years or so later than the first printed book).

**Ehrle, Cardinal Franz**
A scholar of high reputation and an outstanding historian of the
Vatican Library. While yet a priest, and director of the Vatican
Library from 1895-1913, he instituted many significant reforms

for making the contents of the Library more easily available to
the public: he compiled complete catalogues of the manuscripts,
expanded the reading room, and effected the publication of
photographic reproductions of important manuscripts.

Elieser, Rabbi
Introduced printing at Lisbon, Portugal in 1489.

Eliot, Rev. John
Seventy-two rabbis, it is noted, prepared the first Greek
translation of the Old Testament; as many Christians probably
worked upon the Latin version before the printing of the Vulgate
text. But Rev. John Eliot single-handedly translated the entire
Old and New Testaments into the Indian language, a language at
that time unwritten and unknown. The New Testament was completed first and issued with a separate title page dated 1661. It
was later combined and issued with the Old Testament.

Elzivir, Louis (1540-1617)
Founder in the university town of Leyden of one of the most
prosperous familes of printer-publishers in the entire history
of Dutch printing and publishing. The Elzivir family was especially distinguished by the two sons of Louis Elzivir, Abraham
and Bonaventura. Between the foundation of the House of Elzivir
in 1585 and its close in 1712, the firm published over 1,600
separate works, most of which were Latin editions of the
classics, theology, history, medicine, and, to a slighter
degree, French dramatic and literary works.

Enchede, Isaac and Joannes
In 1743 they added a foundry to their printing office, founding
an establishment which carried their family name into the
twentieth century.

Englemann, Godefroi
In 1837 he took out French patents for a method of color lithography which he called "chromo-lithography."

Erasmus, Desiderius (1466?-1536)
He was the greatest author of his time and the first to profit
from the full potentialities of the printing press, through which
his writings gained wide dispersion.

Estienne, Henri (1460-1520)
   Founder of one of the most important families in the history
   of French printing, personally noted for the deep concern he
   evidenced towards the typographical accuracy of his texts.

Estienne, Robert
   The son of Henri Estienne and probably the most illustrious
   printer in the Estienne family. Many of his works were printed
   in fine types designed by Garamonde, and decorated with ornaments, borders, and initials designed by Tory. In his second
   printing of his monumental Latin Thesaurus in 1535, he is said
   to have established the alphabetical order of words as a dictionary method. In 1550, after having published remarkable editions of the Bible in Latin, Hebrew, Greek, and French, and
   correcting many of the errors made by scribes in transcription,
   he brought out the fourth edition of the New Testament. In this
   edition the text is divided into verses for the first time.

Eugene IV, Pope (1431-1447)
   He was instrumental in substantially enlarging the Vatican
   Library.

Evans, Edmund
   Founder of the Raquet Court Press in 1851, he gained fame for
   his color engravings, his production of colored paper book
   covers (used for pasting on to board bindings), and for the
   production of many inexpensive, but attractively colored,
   children's books.

Eve, Nicholas and Clovis
   Nicholas bound books for Henry III; his brother Clovis plied
   his trade during the reigns of Henry IV and Louis XIII. The
   Eves were the only binders of their time to achieve total
   harmony of binding. Their development to a high degree of
   the fanfare style with petit fers (small tools), instead of stamps,
   made for one of the most important changes in the history of
   binding.

Everett, Edward
   He made an important foundation gift of books to the Boston
   Public Library, consisting of state papers and public docu-
   ments complete with a catalogue.

# F

Fanti, Sigismondo

His Theorica et Practica . . . de Modo Scribendi, printed at Venice in 1514, is the first book on the theory of writing and the basis for all other writing books.

Faques

Starting in 1504, he placed on his title pages the term Regius Impressor, providing future students with the earliest record in English bibliography of a Printer to the King.

Favorsky

One of the leaders of Soviet engravers, many books in the twentieth century have been illustrated by him with woodcuts.

Federov

With Mstislavetz, and at the request of Ivan IV, he set up the first Russian press at Moscow in 1563.

Feliciano, Felice

An archaeologist of Verona, in 1463 he composed a treatise on epigraphic lettering, the earliest known critique on letter forms. The only existing copy, a manuscript, is held by the Vatican Library.

Fell, John

Dean of Christ Church, he brought from Holland to the Oxford Press, between the years 1667-1772, the whole range of types and matrices, which are commonly known by his name, together with some learned fonts of oriental faces. From this beginning developed the great University Press, later called Clarendon. The Fell types are still in use at the Clarendon Press.

Feng Tao

In 932 he and his associates presented the memorial which initiated the printing of the Confucian classics, a project successfully concluded in 953, the complete work, text and commentaries, coming to one hundred and thirty volumes. Because of this work, and despite the incontestable evidence of earlier printing in Shu and in the works of Chinese chroniclers, Feng Tao occupies a place in the history of Chinese printing comparable to that held by Gutenberg in Europe. No specimen of the printing initiated by Fen Tao has survived.

## Ferdinand III

Formed his own library at Florence, in the process of which he spared no expense or difficulty. At his death it totaled 40,000 volumes and over 1,000 manuscripts, including the manuscripts of Galileo in eighty-six volumes.

## Ferguson, Robert

One of the pioneer printers of Tennessee. In 1791, with George Roulstone as partner, the first press was set up at Rogersville, Tennessee.

## Ferrandus

In 1474 at Brescia, he printed the first complete text in Greek, Batrachomyomachia.

## Ferrar, Nicholas

Producer of some of the most interesting bindings in England during the reign of Charles I. Among his well known works were: Harmony of the Book of Kings and Chronicles (1637), Harmony (1640), and a Pentateuch (1642), the last two bound and gilt tooled for Charles II.

## Fichet, Guillaume

Professor at the University of the Sorbonne, Paris, he was one of the scholars (the other was Jean Heynlyn) to whom the introduction of printing into France was due. Under the patronage of Fichet and Heynlyn, the first Paris press was set up at the Borbonne by Freiburger, Gering, and Kranz in 1470.

## Field, Haviland

Under his direction a bibliographic bureau was established in the last years of the nineteenth century for the dissemination of information on the natural sciences and to aid in the editing of the bibliographic portions of a number of natural-science periodicals.

Finiguerra, Maso (1426-1464)
A Florentine goldsmith, he is regarded by some (mistakenly) as the inventor of intaglio engraving.

Flandro, Matteo
Establisher of an early Spanish press at Saragossa, he published an edition of the Manipulus Curatorum, the first dated and signed book to be printed in Spain.

Flores, Dona Francisca
In 1720 she introduced printing at Oaxaca, Mexico.

Fogny
In 1582 he printed the Rheims New Testament, the first known Catholic English version.

Force, Peter
The Peter Force Collection of 60,000 volumes of Americana-- books, early newspapers, maps, manuscripts, incunabula, and other materials was purchased by United States Congress (for The Library of Congress) in 1867 for $100,000.

Foster, John
He purchased the press and typographical equipment of Marmaduke Johnson and, starting to print early in 1675, became the first printer in Boston.

Foulis, Andrew and Robert
Excellent Glasgow printers of the early part of the eighteenth century, the two brothers specialized in printing editions of the classics, characterized by exceptional presswork and precision. One of their earliest works was an edition of Horace, now known as the Immaculate. Other representative works include editions of Homer and Sophocles, of Paradise Lost and the poems of Gray and Pope, and a twenty-volume edition of Cicero.

Fourdrinier, Henry
In 1803 he introduced into England a papermaking machine and, during the subsequent years, so dominated the field that the machine is known by his name.

Fournier, Claude
Manager of the Le Bé type foundry and the father of two more famous sons, Jean Pierre Fournier and Pierre Simon Fournier.

Fournier, Jean Pierre  A skilled engraver and punch cutter who added to his reputation by acquiring a remarkable collection of punches and types from the leading European foundries and founders, including several by Granjon and Garamonde.

Fournier, Pierre Simon  Born in Paris in 1712, he gained fame for his type emblems, ornamented letters, and type borders, all of which he effected with taste and skill; but he is best known for his works on printing, the most important of which were: Tables des Proportions (1737), Môdeles des Caractères de l'Imprimerie (1742), and Manuel Typographique (1764). The Manuel Typographique is one of the most important treatises on punch cutting and typecasting ever written, covering the entire technique of punch cutting and matrix making, the aesthetic principles relating to the choice of type for special purposes, information about European foundries, and a comprehensive selection of type specimens.

Fowle, Daniel
Set up the first press at New Hampshire in 1756.

Francis I
In 1530 he presented the office of Imprimeur du Roi to Tory; in 1535 he issued an edict prescribing the death penalty for the unauthorized printing of books.

Francois, Jean Charles (1717-1769)
He claimed to have experimented in the crayon method as early as 1740, and he is generally looked upon as the inventor of the process.

Franklin, Benjamin
Generally credited with the establishment of the first American subscription library in Philadelphia in 1731. In 1882 his manuscript papers and the volumes known as the Franklin Collection were acquired by the Library of Congress.

## Franklin, James

Older brother and one time master of the printing trade of Benjamin Franklin, he introduced printing at Rhode Island.

## Frederick II

In the thirteenth century, the roman cursive having by this time become illegible, he prohibited its further use.

## Frederick III

Founder of the Royal Library in the Castle of Copenhagen. During the years 1661-1664 he acquired the valuable libraries formerly belonging to three Danish noblemen, collections rich in foreign literature, principally French, Italian, and Spanish. Among the works in King Frederick's library was a priceless collection of ancient Icelandic literature.

## Froben, Johann

A German printer who set up his press at Basil in 1491. He was one of the first publishers to evidence real esteem for the value of an author's work. He not only paid Erasmus author-ship fees, but he also gave him a retaining salary for his work as a proofreader and editor. Holbein illustrated many of the works of Froben and, through the latter's assistance, later took up residence in England under the patronage of Henry VIII.

## Fust, Johann

Fifteenth-century citizen of Mainz, reputed by his grandson, Johann Schoeffer, to be the first author of the art of printing. When he took over the printing establishment from Gutenberg in its entirety he also took over Schoeffer's services (originally employed by Gutenberg as a typesetter and proofreader). The first known publication of the Fust and Schoeffer office was a Psalter, 1457, the first book with a printing date and the name of the printers. Fust and Schoeffer in 1463 printed a Papal Bull of Pius II, the earliest known example of a printed title upon a protective leaf.

# G

Garamond, Claude
One of the earliest and most famous of all the French type
designers. Under the patronage of François I he produced his
famous Grec du Roi, three Greek types on the handwriting of
the calligrapher Angelas Vergetias; he also designed several
sizes of roman and italic types, the success of which led to a
decline in the use of the Gothic letter.

Garnett, Porter
In 1923 he set up the Laboratory Press at Carnegie Institute
of Technology, Pittsburgh, Pennsylvania, which is probably
the first purely private press devoted to the ends of education
in fine printing.

Ged, William
An Edinburgh goldsmith, his name is most often associated
with the invention of stereotyping. He formed a partnership
with William Fenner, a London stationer, and Thomas James,
an English typefounder; together they obtained from Cambridge
University the privilege of printing Bibles and prayer books by
the Ged method. The attempt proved futile, however, and in
the process Ged met with so much opposition that in the end
he was ruined and returned to Scotland.

Gelasius, Pope
In 494 he authorized the list of proscribed books, the earliest
known instance of such a prohibition.

Geminus
In 1545 he published at London an edition of Vesalius' Anatomy
with a splendid title page and impressive full-page anatomical
plates. This work, while creating a fashion for elaborate books,
provided an impetus to the development of intaglio illustrations.

George I
In 1715 he presented to the Cambridge University Library the
collection of John Moore, Bishop of Ely, containing 30,755

volumes, including 1,790 manuscripts, a presentation which at the time more than doubled the possessions of the library.

**George IV**
In 1823 he gave to the British Museum the Royal Library, a great part of which had been collected by George III, one of only several English kings who collected books extensively.

**Gerbert, Martin**
A famous bibliophile, he made the first description of a Gutenberg Bible in 1765, based on the Vollbehr copy now in the Library of Congress.

**Gerson**
His Collectorium super Magnificat, printed at Esslingen by Fyner in 1473, is the earliest book known to contain printed musical notes.

**Gesner, Conrad**
His Bibliotheca Universalis, printed at Zurich by Froschauer in 1545-1555, is the most notable early attempt to catalogue an entire realm of printed books. Because of this work he is generally regarded as "The Father of Bibliography."

**Gibbings, Robert and Moira**
In January 1924 they purchased the Golden Cockerel Press and brought out thereafter many of the handsomest books illustrated with wood engravings by Robert Gibbings himself, Eric Gill, and young artists of exceptional talent.

**Gifford, Reverend Andrew (1700-1784)**
The Museum's first numismatist and the first member of the staff of the British Museum to be a collector of antiquities (coins, books, manuscripts, pictures, and "curiosities").

**Gill, Eric (1882-1940)**
An outstanding type designer of the early twentieth century, known especially for his famous Gill Sans Serif type, which is particularly suited for display and job printing. His most successful book type is his Perpetua, designed for the Monotype Corporation in 1929.

Gillis, Walt (1855-1925)
An important, influential American printer who produced the first number of Vogue in Caslon type and thereby effected a revival of the type in this country. In 1906-1907 the Gillis Press printed the celebrated Don Quixote, illustrated by Vierge, leading Spanish artist.

Gilmore, Thomas
In 1764 he and William Brown introduced printing in Quebec.

Giron, Mariana Valdes Tellez
Introduced printing at Guadalajara, Mexico in 1792.

Giunta Family: Luca (d. 1537), Filippo (d. 1517), Bernardo (d. 1551)
An important Italian family of printers that flourished in three countries from 1482 to 1642. The Giunta family was the main publishing rival of Aldus Manutius; among its publications were fine illustrated works and books of Church music.

Glover, Reverend Jose
He may be regarded as the father of printing in the United States, for at his direction a printing house was established by (probably) Matthew Day (also spelled Daye) at Cambridge, Massachusetts in 1639.

Goddard, William
He set up a press at Baltimore in 1773 and later created the American postal system.

Gorton, Abraham
In February 1475, he completed the printing of Solomon ben Isaac's Perusch ha tora (a commentary on the Pentatech), the second earliest work in which Hebrew type is used (earliest use was in Arba Turim, 1474).

Goudy, Frederick W. (1865-1947)
A very prolific designer of typefaces. Of the more than one hundred different fonts of type which he designed, the best known are the Kennerley, Goudy Modern, and Goudy Newstyle. In 1903 he founded the Village Press, an American private press of distinction.

Goupil

The first successful applier of color gravure (Paris, 1870's), a process which was soon afterwards introduced into America by the Rembrandt Intaglio Company.

Goya, Francisco (1746-1828)

Noted for the effects which he obtained through a combination of the processes of etching and aquatint. His most brilliant work was a set of eighty-two plates known as the Desastres de la Guerra, done during the French occupation of Spain, but not published until 1863.

Graf, Urs (c. 1485-1529)

A Swiss goldsmith and engraver, he was the first successful employer of the white-line method. His "Girl Bathing Her Feet," made probably in 1513, is the earliest extant dated etching in Europe.

Grafton, Richard

An English printer of the sixteenth century. In association with Whitchurch, he produced an edition of Coverdale's Bible which, dedicated by Thomas Matthews to Henry VIII, is often referred to as the Matthews Bible. In 1543 Grafton and Whitchurch were granted a Royal License for the printing of service books and, later, for the printing of primers.

Grandjean, Philippe (1666-1732)

In 1692 he was commissioned by Louis XIV to produce a new series of types for the exclusive use of the Imprimerie Royale. Begun in 1693 the task was completed in 1745, thirteen years after Grandjean's death. The types, known as the Romains du Roi, consisted of eighty-two complete fonts: twenty-one different bodies of italic and twenty different bodies of italic capitals. These types, virtually the first modern face, had far reaching influence.

Granjon, Robert

French sixteenth-century publisher, printer, type cutter, and typefounder, he is best known for his so-called Civilité types, which he introduced at Lyons in 1557. They are probably the earliest script types, named for their early use in La Civilité Puerile by Erasmus, printed by Tavernier, Antwerp, in 1559.

Green, Bernard R.
Supervised the completion of the plans for, and the erection of, the Library of Congress.

Green, Samuel
He took over the press of Matthew Day upon his death. His first major work was the edition of the Bible in native Indian dialect, conceived by Reverend John Eliot. In 1704 he printed the Boston News Letter, the first American newspaper.

Green, Valentine (1739-1813)
A distinguished English Mezzotinter. He was appointed associate engraver to the Royal Academy and mezzotint engraver to George III.

Gregoriis Brothers
Fifteenth-century Venetian printers whose printed book illustrations brought the art to new heights. Their printing of Ketham's Fasciculus Medicine, with an illustration colored by stencil (1493), is one of the earliest known instances of the use of the stencil method in colored illustration.

Gregory II, Pope
In 716 he was presented with a fresh transcript of the Vulgate Bible, now known as the Codex Amiatinus and considered the best manuscript of the Latin Vulgate. It is preserved in the Laurentian Library.

Grenville, Thomas (1755-1846)
An English collector whose library, although small, was unsurpassed in quality, including almost every subject, but specializing in early Americana, incunabula, and the classics. In 1847 he bequeathed the library to the British Museum, where it remains as one of the very special collections.

Grolier, Jean
A French scholar, statesman, and famous book collector (born in 1479). Many of his collection of over 8,000 books had bindings which bore the legend Il Grolierii et Amicorum (For Jean Grolier and his friends), bindings characterized by interlacing strapwork decorated with arabesque foliage enclosed within gilt lines; hence the term Grolier bindings. The

Grolieresque was directly or indirectly the ancestor of almost all ornate bindings for two centuries.

Gryphius, Sebastian (1493-1556)
A great printer at Lyons, he printed between 1528 and 1556 one thousand books in French, Greek, Hebrew, Italian, and Latin. In 1550 he brought out his monumental Latin Bible, the largest up to then in size of type and format.

Guillard, Charlotte
One of the earliest known woman master printers. During the second half of the sixteenth century, she issued many celebrated Greek and Latin editions of the Fathers of the Church.

Gutenberg, John (c. 1398-1468)
Generally accepted as the inventor of printing, although there is some disagreement as to whether or not he was the sole originator of the practice. According to twentieth-century investigations, in 1445 he completed his three principal printing inventions: (1) the press itself, capable of printing on both sides of the sheet; (2) the adjustable type mold for casting separate alphabetical letters, large or small, in accurate alignment; and (3) the viscous ink required by metallic printing surfaces.

# H

Hacket, John
Bishop of Coventry and Lichfield, in 1670 he bequeathed 1,000 volumes to the Cambridge University Library.

Hadrianus, Cornelius (1521-1588)
His Batavia, printed posthumously at Leyden in 1588, contains the earliest, much discussed record of the Caster tradition.

Haebler, Konrad (1857-1946)
With the publication of his Typenrepertorium der Wiegendrucke at Leipzig in 1905, he made an important contribution to the study of incunabula types.

Hagar, George
In 1682 he was granted a patent in England for his method of adding size to the pulp in the vat instead of applying it by hand to the finished sheets.

Hahn, Ulrich
A Bavarian, invited by Cardinal Turrecremata to come to Rome, he was the second printer in Italy. His first work, an edition of Turrecremata's Meditationes De Vita Christi, published in 1467, was illustrated with thirty-four crude woodcuts, the first to appear in any book printed in Italy.

Hain, Ludwig
With the publication of his Reportorium bibliographicum (1826-1834), it may be said that modern bibliography of incunabula began; for in this monumental work, Hain describes in detail all the incunabula known at the time (16, 299).

Hallervord
A Königsberg philologist, his Bibliotheca Curiosa, prepared in 1676, has the distinction of being the first critical bibliography.

Halliwell, J. O. (1820-1889)
An eminent English book collector of the late nineteenth century. His private library was particularly rich in Elizabethan works. In later years he gave generously of his holdings to libraries in England and America. When his library was finally sold, most of the Shakespeare material went to the Folger Library in Washington.

Han (Hahn), Ulrich
The first printer to print musical notes and text in black and then, by a second impression (often in another color), to add the staff. This he did in a missal printed for the Roman curia in October 1476. (See Hahn above.)

Harkness, Mrs. E. S.
In 1926 she presented a copy of the Gutenberg Bible to the Yale University Library, which she purchased for $126,000.00.

**Harvard, John**

In 1638 he founded the first university library in the United States.

**Haultin**

In 1527 he printed a collection of songs in four voices in which he used a method designed by him, printing the stave and notes in one impression.

**Häuy, Valentin (1745-1822)**

In 1784 at Paris he invented the method of printing in relief for the blind.

**Hedin**

In 252 A.D. his expedition discovered at Loulan the earliest clearly dated paper which was used for documents.

**Henry VIII**

In 1536 he dissolved the English monasteries, an act which prompted patrons and scholars to collect books in order that they might be preserved. In 1538 he prohibited the importation of English books printed abroad.

**Herford, John**

A well known English printer of the sixteenth century. One of his better known works was an edition of Lydgate's Lyfe and Passion of Seint Albon, apparently printed at the request of Robert Catton, abbot of the monastery.

**Hess, Andreas**

In 1473 he printed a work in Budapest which makes him the first printer in Hungary.

**Heynlyn, Jean**

A professor at the University of the Sorbonne, Paris, who, with another professor at the same university (Guillaume Fichet by name), is credited with being the ultimate introducer of printing into France.

**Hibbert, George (1757-1837)**

The Book of Orphic Hymns, printed by Hibbert at his private press at London in 1827, marked one of the earliest attempts to reform Greek types and to produce an experimental face.

Hildegard, Charles
   In 1665 he was granted a patent for the manufacture of blue
   sugar paper.

Hochfelder, Caspar
   Set up the first press at Cracow, Poland in 1475.

Hoe, Richard March (1812-1886)
   Regarded by some as the real developer of the rotary press in
   1846. In 1856 he installed at London the first printing machine
   of the kind bearing his name, used to produce Lloyd's Weekly
   Newspaper.

Hoe, Robert (1839-1909)
   One of the founders of the Grolier Club and one of America's
   outstanding book collectors. His principal interest was in rare
   books and fine bindings of which, as early as 1896, he possessed 8,000. When the collection was sold after his death
   it brought over two million dollars.

Holbein, Hans
   A great master of the woodcut, he produced over three hundred
   designs for book decoration during his lifetime. Two of his
   great pieces of book work done between 1519 and 1526 were:
   Dance of Death and Icones Historiarum Veteris Testamenti.

Holle, Leonhard
   An outstanding fifteenth-century printer at Ulm. His edition of
   Ptolemy's Cosmographia (1482) was the first book with wood-
   cup maps.

Hornby, C. H. St. John
   He founded the Ashendene Press in 1894, using at first the
   Subiaco type. Among its great productions was a Dante in 1909.
   By 1919 it had printed thirty-nine major pieces and was the
   oldest and best of the existing private presses.

Horne
   In 1909 he established at London the Ricardi Press and designed
   a typeface which he called by the same name.

Hullmandel, Charles Joseph (1789-1850)
   His discovery of the lithotint method in 1840 opened the field for
   further experiments in color lithography.

Huntington, Henry E.

In 1919 he founded the Henry E. Huntington Library, the only library in America which compares with the libraries of the Old World in the possession of incunabula and manuscript material.

Hurus Brothers

They were the first to introduce a printer's device into Spanish books. The Spanish press established by Pablo and Juan Hurus at Saragossa in the early part of the fifteenth century flourished for over three-quarters of a century.

Huth, Alfred H. (1850-1910)

Son of Henry Huth, he added to the collection which his father began. When the Huth Library was finally sold it brought over three hundred thousand pounds, perhaps the most that was ever realized from the sale of a single collection.

Huth, Henry

A well known English book collector and bibliographer of the late nineteenth century.

# I

Image and Horne

From 1886 to 1892 they issued a handsome folio magazine The Hobby Horse, which excited keen interest in the format of literary periodicals.

Isadore, Bishop of Seville (600-636)

A Spanish scholar who not only collected a library of the best literature of his day, but also drew from it to compose an early version of an encyclopedia.

Ives, Frederick

He is generally regarded as the inventor of a practical halftone process.

# J

Jackson, John Baptist
An eighteenth-century English wood engraver who studied color work in Paris, Rome, and Venice, and using six to ten blocks for each print obtained interesting results in his work. His Essay on Engraving and Printing in Chiaroscuro is a historically significant work.

James, Thomas
The first keeper of the library which later was named the Bodleian, a post he held until 1620. His value to the library in personal services and in gifts of books was noteworthy.

Janinet, François (1752-1813)
One of the first to successfully use the aquatint process. His work, in which he employed as many as eight separate color plates successively printed in register for each print, was of consistently superior quality.

Jefferson, Thomas
The purchase of his collection of some 6,000 books by Congress marked the real beginning of the Library of Congress.

Jenkinson, Francis (1853-1923)
A distinguished entomologist and scholar, he carried on the task, begun by Henry Bradshaw, of historically classifying the books in the Cambridge University Library.

Jenson, Nicholas
The first attempt to establish a press in France was made in 1458 when he was bidden by Charles VII to go to Mainz to learn about the craft of printing and then to return to set up a press at Paris. Regarded by many today as the first non-German printer, he printed his first book at Venice in 1470, the De Praeparatione Evangelica by Eusebius. In this he employed one of the most beautiful and influential roman faces ever designed. In 1471 he printed at Venice the Decor Puellarum, one of the earliest (if not the earliest) book of etiquette.

Jerome, Saint

During the years 383-405, he translated the Bible from Hebrew and Greek into Latin. Known as the Vulgate it superseded by 800 all other earlier translations. It is extant in no less than 8,000 manuscripts.

John of Verona

In 1472 he printed with large initials in heavy gold upon colored backgrounds the first edition of Valturius' De Re Militari, a work celebrated for its wood engravings.

John of Westphalia

Also known as John of Paderborn, he was one of the first (1473) to print in the Southern Netherlands.

Johnston, James

In 1763 he set up a press at Savannah, Georgia, the first ever to be established in Georgia.

John the Good

His grant to the University of Paris in 1354 of tax-free mills at Essones is an early instance of the encouragement of the industry by royalty.

Jones, Owen (1809-1874)

In Plans, Elevations, Sections, and Details of the Alambra, which appeared in 1836, are found the first successful book illustrations in color lithography.

Jugge, Richard

One time senior Queen's Printer to Elizabeth, he was responsible for the printing of the first edition of the famous Bishop's Bible (1569). Like Coverdale's 1535 edition, it is also known as the Treacle.

Junius, Hadrianus

In his Batavia, written in 1568, but not published until 1588, he gave a long account of the invention of printing, in which he named Caster as the first printer.

# K

Keller, Friedrich Gottlob (1816-1895)
A German who is credited by some with the invention in 1840 of mechanical wood pulp.

Ketelaer, Nicolaus
One of two printers who were responsible for an edition of Comestor's Historia Scholastica, printed at Utrecht in 1473, the first dated and signed book to appear in Holland.

Kieberg and Bauer
Builders of the first steam press in London in 1812.

Kirgate, Thomas
An excellent printer, he filled the role of printer and secretary for Horace Walpole, founder of the Strawberry Hill Press.

Kirkhall, Edward
The first English exponent of chiaroscuro (early eighteenth century). Using mezzotint and etching, he combined intaglio and relief methods in producing single prints.

Knight, Charles
A pioneer of illustrated magazine literature, he patented in 1838 a special color-printing method called "illuminated printing," which allowed a picture to be done in four or more colors.

Koberger, Anthony
One of the most successful printer-publishers of the fifteenth century, labelled by some as the first captain of the printing industry: owner of at least sixteen bookshops; employer of at least one hundred printers; operator of some twenty-four separate presses; dispatcher of book-selling agents to many cities in Germany and elsewhere. Among the works printed and published by Koberger were: Schatbehalter (1491), Liber Chronicanum (1493), and the Nuremberg Chronicle (1493). In 1480 he sent out a circular, the earliest printed advertising piece known.

Koblinger, Stephan
   The first printer in Austria (Vienna, 1482).

Koelhoff, Johann the Elder
   A printer at Cologne from 1472 to 1493. In 1472 he printed an
   edition of Nider's Praeceptorium Divinae Legis, in which he
   was the first to introduce printed signatures on each section
   of the book to guide the binder.

Koenig, Friedrich
   He invented the Cylinder Press in 1812. This was first put to
   use by the London Times in 1814. In 1814 Koenig introduced a
   glue and molasses compound to be used on press rollers in place
   of buckskin.

Korf, Count M. A.
   He was librarian of the Russian Imperial Library from 1849 to
   1861. During his administration the library acquired 350,000
   volumes and 11,000 manuscripts, not to mention an appreciable
   number of prints, photographs, musical scores, and maps.

Korin, Ogata (1653? - 1716)
   One of the best of the seventeenth-century Japanese illustrators.
   Comparable to him, in the nineteenth century, are Hokusai and
   Hiroshige and, in the twentieth century, Kitigawa Utamaro.

Krantz, Martin (fl. 1462 - 1478)
   In 1470 he and two others set up the first Paris press at the
   Sorbonne. The first work produced was the Epistolae of
   Gasparinus, set in roman type.

Kravchenko
   A leading Russian illustrator and wood engraver of the twentieth
   century. In 1928 he was awarded first prize at the Ten Years
   of Graphic Arts in the U.S.S.R. Exhibition.

Kromberger, Jacob
   A partner of Stanislaus, one of the founders of the press in
   1491 at Seville. By 1504 the Seville press was entirely in
   Kromberger's hands. In 1527 the Kromberger Press at Seville
   came into the control of his son John Kromberger.

# L

**Lair, John**
A native of Siegburg, near Cologne, he is the first known printer
at Cambridge, nine of his works being printed between 1521 and
1522. His first book was printed in 1521; his second book, Cuius-
dam Fidelis Christiani Epistolae ad Christianos Omnes, was
the first English book to contain Greek characters printed from
movable types.

**Lanston, Tolbert**
In 1887 he invented the Monotype, a typecasting machine with
two separate units, a keyboard and a caster.

**Laud, Archbishop**
Chancellor of the University of Oxford from 1630 to 1641, he
obtained a Royal Letters Patent for the University in 1630,
which allowed it the services of three printers, each of whom
could use two presses and have in his employ two apprentices.

**Lavalliere, Duke Louis de**
An outstanding eighteenth-century collector of books, he built
up one of the largest private libraries ever found, including
rare books, fine bindings, manuscripts, and complete collections.
At his death in 1784, his library exceeded 100,000 items.

**Le Blon, J. C. (1667-1741)**
The first mezzotinter in color whose work can be given a definite
date, he formulated the notion that all gradations of color are
reducible to three primary colors--red, blue, and yellow. He
thus made three plates for every print, inked them separately,
and printed them successively in register.

**Leempt, Gerard de**
One of the printers (the other was Nichlaus Ketelaer) responsible
for the appearance in Holland of the first dated and signed book,
an edition of Comestor's Historia Scholastica, printed at Utrecht
in 1473.

## Leeu, Gerard

The first printer at Gouda, in 1480 he printed a book of fables Dyalogus creaturarum, in which woodcuts made their first appearance as book illustrations. The work proved very popular and many editions, in Latin and Dutch, were subsequently brought out in the Netherlands.

## Legate, John

In 1628 he printed for Henry Featherstone, a book importer, what is regarded as the first English classified catalogue of foreign books available for sale in England.

## Leighton, Archibald

In 1825 he made available to publishers and bookbinders a sized cloth for bookbinding purposes, the first time this had ever been done.

## Leighton, George

Noted for his colored supplements to the Illustrated London News, in which he employed a method quite different from that of Baxter, for whom he once worked as an apprentice: he used wood-engraved blocks for his outlines and then added his color from etched or aquatinted plates.

## Lenox, James

He brought the first Gutenberg Bible to America in 1847.

## Leo X, the Medici Pope (1513-1521)

He made Rome a center of the world of letters, he greatly enlarged the Vatican Library, and he is responsible for preserving the Laurentian Collection.

## Leo XIII

He was the first pope to open to research workers the treasures of the papal archives.

## Le Prince, Jean Baptiste (1734-1781)

He was probably the first to use an aquatint ground consistently with any degree of success; hence, although occasional prints were produced before his time, he may be regarded as the inventor of the process.

Le Roy, Guillaume
In 1475 he published at Lyons an Exposition of the Bible, with
a woodcut at the front of each book, the first appearance of
woodcut in a French book. Le Roy also has the distinction of
being the first printer at Paris. (Le Roy is the French form
of the printer's real name, Wilhelm König.)

Le Talleur
In 1490 he printed Littleton's Tonores Novelli and Statham's
Abridgment of Cases in a thin slanting type, neither roman
nor Gothic., a kind of forerunner of italic.

Leto, Guillaume Pomponio (1425-1498)
One of the finest fifteenth-century calligraphers and founder of
the Roman Academy, he produced between 1470 and 1498 exceptional editions of classic authors.

Lettou, John (John of Lithuania)
Caxton's principal rival, he set up a press at Westminster in
1479-1480 and soon thereafter (probably in 1480) printed an
edition of the Quaestiones of Antonius Andreae, the first double-
column book printed in England.

Levy, Max
The perfection of the halftone process depended upon the
development of a cross-ruled screen. Max Levy of Philadelphia
constructed a ruling machine suitable for the ruling of satisfactory screens.

Lignamine, Johannes Phillippus de
In completing the Chronica Summorum, which was begun by
Riccobaldus of Ferrara and published at Rome in 1474, de
Lignamine made the first historical reference to printing,
naming both Gutenberg and Fust as skilled in printing on
parchment.

Lintot, Bernard
An outstanding English publisher of the eighteenth century. In
1712 he published his Miscellany, containing verses of Gay,
Swift, and others. In 1714 he published a second edition, which
contained Pope's Rape of the Lock and other early verses. In
1718 he published Pope's Iliad; in 1725, his Odyssey.

**Logan, James**
A chief justice and later lieutenant governor of Pennsylvania,
he possessed the most impressive private library of the middle colonies, some 3,000 volumes, strong in mathematics,
astronomy, and science and, to a lesser degree, the classics.

**London, William**
A seventeenth-century bookseller known mainly for his catalogues: Catalogue of the most vendible Books in England (1657),
a list of 3,096 works covering a range of subjects; A Catalogue
of New Books, by Way of Supplement to the former (1660), a
list of 396 additional works.

**Longepierre, Bernard de Requeleyne, Baron de (1659-1721)**
A scholar, translator, and celebrated book collector. Many
of his books had bindings decorated with the emblem of the
Golden Fleece. Even Boyet and Padeloup executed fine bindings
for him.

**Lottin, Augustin Martin (1726-1793)**
In 1789 appeared his Catalogue Chronologique des Librairies
et des Libraires-Imprimeurs de Paris, a work which took
thirty-six years of preparation and six years of revision and
printing.

**Louffen, De**
In 1470 he printed the Mammotrectus of Marchesinus, a work
which explains the difficult words of the Bible to parish priests.
This is the first dated book of what was in the fifteenth-century
Switzerland.

**Louis XIV**
In 1640 he founded the Imprimerie Royale and made Sebastien
Cramoisy the first director; in 1692 he ordered the creation
of a new series of types for exclusive use of the Imprimerie
Royale. Grandjean was chosen to execute the recommendations.

**Louis XII**
In 1513 he issued an edict extolling printing and exempting it
from heavy impost, an act for which many regard him as the
"Father of Letters."

Low, Sampson
> An English bookseller and noted publisher of annual book cata-
> logues from 1845 to 1860. In 1853 the title was <u>A</u> <u>Catalogue</u> <u>of</u>
> <u>Books</u> <u>published</u> <u>in</u> <u>the</u> <u>United</u> <u>Kingdom</u> <u>during</u> <u>the</u> <u>year</u> . . .;
> after 1853 the title was <u>The</u> <u>British</u> <u>Catalogue</u> <u>of</u> <u>Books</u>.

Lucas, van Leyden (1494-1533)
> With the publication in 1571 of his writing book, he be-
> came a predominant influence in Spanish calligraphy.

Luce
> Between 1740 and 1770 he designed a series of types which,
> because of their slimness, were adapted to the setting of
> longer lines of poetry; they came to be styled "poetique."

Lupton, T. E. (1791-1873)
> For his discovery of the method of giving a copperplate a
> steel surface by electro-deposition, by which he was able to
> combine the advantages of copper with the durability of steel,
> he was awarded the Isis Medal of the Royal Society of Arts.

Luther, Martin (1483-1546)
> In 1522 his German New Testament was printed at Wittenberg;
> in 1534, his Bible in German was printed at Wittenberg.

Luttrell, Edward
> An Irishman who settled in London and acquired a reputation
> as a portraitist in crayon.

# M

McArdell, James
> One of the most brilliant mezzotint engravers of the eighteenth
> century, noted for his plates after Rubens, Vandyck, Rembrandt,
> and Murillo, but known best for those after Sir Joshua Reynolds.

Machlinia, William de
A one-time partner of John Lettou (John of Lithuania), Caxton's chief rival. He was the first printer to produce an English book with a separate printed title page. When he ceased printing in 1490-1491, his business was taken over by Pynson.

Mahon, Charles
The Third Earl of Stanhope, in 1800 he invented a new printing press in which an iron framework was substituted for the wooden body of the old press, and in which the platen was twice the size of that which had been used before, thus permitting a larger sheet to be printed.

Makario
A monk who introduced the first press in 1494 in Rieka, in Montenegro.

Maler, Bernhard
A fifteenth-century printer at Venice, a partner of Erhard Ratdolt and Peter Löslein, by whom were introduced several important innovations in book production: the first decorative title page; the first use of gold ink for printing; probably the first printing in several different colors.

Malton, Thomas (1708-1894)
One of the most important late eighteenth-century artists in aquatint.

Mansion, Colard (?-1484)
In 1476 he printed at Bruges De la Ruine des Nobles Homnes, a French edition of Boccaccio, evidencing perhaps the first use of intaglio illustration in a printed book.

Manutius, Aldus
The first of a well known sixteenth-century Italian family of printers that gained fame for their texts of classical and Italian authors. His name also appears as Aldo Manuzio.

Marchant
In 1485, using a series of woodcuts, he produced the first printed Dance of Death.

**Marschalk, Andrew**
A printer and army officer, he introduced printing at Walnut Hills, near Natchez, Mississippi about the year 1798.

**Materot**
A penman in the papal office at Avignon, whose writing manual appeared in 1608, immediately following which the open, running lettre italienne bastarde gained in popularity while the slower secretarial hands fell gradually into disuse.

**Mather, Cotton**
An author and minister whose library was probably the largest in New England in the later seventeenth century, containing before his death some 4,000 volumes.

**Matthiasson**
In 1534 he printed the Breviarium Holense at Holar, the first book printed in Iceland.

**Matthieu, Thomas**
A famous French book collector (long thought to be an Italian and better known perhaps by the name of Thomasso Maioli). Many of the bindings in his library were decorated with inter-lacing strapwork, tooled either with outline or azured tools.

**Maunsell, Andrew (?-1595)**
His Catalogue of English Printed Books (1595) was the first published in England.

**Maximilian, Emperor**
In 1512 he commissioned leading artists of the day, such as Durer, Hans Burkmaier, Albrecht Altdorfer, and Hans Schau-felein to work upon a series of ambitious woodcut projects, the main one being a triumphal arch printed from ninety-two separate blocks, measuring ten feet and six inches by nine feet, and a procession printed from one hundred and thirty-eight separate blocks, measuring over two hundred feet when fully extended.

**Maynard, Robert A.**
A director until 1931 of the Gregynog Press, established in 1922 at Gregynog, near Newtown, Montgomeryshire. With Horace W. Bray, he produced most of the wood engravings with which the Gregynog books were illustrated.

Mazarin, Cardinal

In 1642 his private book collection was opened as a public library, with Naudé, a well known bibliographer in charge.

Mearne, Samuel

Royal bookbinder for Charles II of England, during his tenure he introduced several effective binding styles: many in morocco, unornamented except for a central gilt-tooled coat of arms; a series of small bindings in black morocco with gold tooling and inlays of red, yellow, and white leather; several in the so-called Mearne Rectangular style.

Medici, Casimo de

He was responsible for what later became the Laurentian Library.

Medici, Piero de

Father of Lorenzo the Magnificent, who really brought the Laurentian Library to its high position.

Meigret, Louis (c.1510-c.1560)

A member of the Pleiade group of poets, in 1542 he constructed the first regular system of phonetic spelling.

Meisenbach, George

He invented the halftone process in 1881 and introduced it into England in 1884.

Mentelin, Johann

He established the first press at Strassburg, perhaps as early as 1458; he was the first German printer to use a type with roman tendencies; he was the first German printer to issue lengthy descriptions of his books. In 1466 he printed at Strassburg a German translation of the Vulgate, the earliest Bible in any modern language, and the first of eighteen editions before Luther's.

Mergenthaler, Ottman

In 1885 he patented the Linotype, a typesetting and typecasting machine which casts slugs (whole lines of type). The Linotype was put into practical use for the first time in 1886 at the office of the New York Herald Tribune.

**Mesplet, Fleury**
A Frenchman, he was the first printer at Montreal. His first
work, printed in 1777, was entitled <u>Officium in Honorem Domini
Nostri J. C.</u> His second work was a newspaper, printed entirely
in French, the <u>Gazette Litteraire</u>.

**Mey, J. Vander**
He is credited with making the first application of the stereotype principle (during the sixteenth century). A similar method
was used at Paris in the seventeenth century; but stereotype
printing was not fully developed until the eighteenth century.

**Michelangelo, Buonarroti (1475-1564)**
He designed the Laurentian Library building.

**Mill**
In 1714 he recorded in England his invention and patent of the
typewriter.

**Milton, John (1608-1674)**
In 1644 he delivered before the English Parliament his speech
<u>Areopagitica</u>, in which he attacked censorship of the press and,
in defiance of a restraining order, had the protest published
without license.

**Moreau, Pierre**
A Parisian writing master and printer. He designed raised letters for the use of the blind, and he was the first to design
script types as such for major typographical uses. In 1643 he
published his first book of these characters, an octavo <u>Imitation
of Christ,</u> dedicated to the queen of Louis XIV.

**Morel, Eugene**
By his activities and writing he made an attempt in 1904 to
introduce in France the American and English notion of the
public library.

**Morgan, John Pierpont (1837-1913)**
A financier who, especially in later years, acquired many of
the finest books in the world (rare books and manuscripts) often
from old English and European family libraries which had
existed for centuries.

Morgan, John Pierpont, Jr.
John Pierpont Morgan, probably more than anyone else, helped
America to become the greatest book-collecting country in the
world and, more perhaps than anyone else in America, exempted
himself from the general antagonism of Englishmen to American
collectors by making it a practice never to bid against the British
Museum on any item which he felt should become a part of it.
John Pierpont Morgan, Jr., continued in his father's footsteps,
extending services to book lovers and cooperating with the
British Museum to secure famous manuscripts.

Morris, William
He founded the Kelmscott Press in 1891 and displayed a true
genius for design. His first typeface was roman, but he then
returned to Gothic for richer effect. Much subsequent fine
printing is due largely to him.

Moseley, Humphrey
Probably the most notable publisher of poetry and literature in
his lifetime: the publisher of Milton's works, publishing the
poet's first collection in 1646; the publisher of the works of
contemporaries, such as Shirley and Davenant.

Moxon, Joseph
In 1683 he provided the first clear information concerning the
origins of type manufacture. He described a type mold in support of the hypothesis that the primitive type mold was prismatic,
rather than slab like.

Moyllus
His Alphabetum, published at Parma in 1480, is the earliest
known printed treatise on the formation of letters.

Mullaby
In 1891 he and Bullock took out a British patent for aluminum
lithoplates.

Murray, John II (1778-1843)
An outstanding figure in the publishing world of nineteenth-
century England. He published Byron's Childe Harold in 1812
(and enjoyed a life-long friendship with the poet); he published
the famous Quarterly Review; he published much of Crabbe's
verse. In 1807 he purchased from Constable a share in Scott's

Marmion; in 1826, however, when Scott faced financial difficulties following the bankruptcy of Constable & Company,
Murray returned to Scott the share in Marmion.

Mychell, John
He began his printing career in London and then moved to
Canterbury where, between 1549 and 1556, he printed eleven
books, the first being an edition of the Psalms, of which there
is only one known copy extant.

Myllar, Andrew
He and Walter Chepman established the first press at Edinburgh,
Scotland, in 1508. Among the earliest works of these two printers
were eleven popular Scottish and English romances, most of
them printed in 1508, copies of which are preserved in the National Library of Scotland.

# N

Nachmias, David and Samuel ibn
They set up the first press in 1494 in Constantinople.

Neumeister
He was the first printer of Dante's Commedia (1472). In 1487
he published his Lyons Missal; in this the French pointed Gothic
type was used very effectively.

Niccoli, Nice di (1363-1437)
On a bequest by him a public library was founded at Florence
in 1437, which later became known as the Laurentian Library,
the oldest existing library in Europe today.

Niccolò di Lorenzo
In 1476 (or 1477) he printed at Florence, Bettini's Monte Sancto

di <u>Dio</u>, which contains the first known copper-engraved illustrations printed directly on the text page.

### Nicholas V, Pope

He may be regarded as the founder of the Vatican Library (1447). When Constantinople fell, he directed the acquisition of some of the treasures of the Imperial Library and invited the exiled Byzantine scholars to Rome, where he commissioned them to translate Greek classics into Latin for the papal library.

### Nicholson, William

In 1790 he took out a patent for a machine which later came to be called a rotary press. He did not, however, embody the plan he had in an actual press. This remained for others to do somewhat later.

### Niepce, de Saint'-Victor (1805-1870)

A partner of Daquerre in the invention of photography in 1824, he made the first engraving on metal by photography in 1826. On this invention all later production of printing surfaces for illustrations have depended. In 1839 he announced, through the Royal Society in London, his discovery of the light sensitive properties of bichromate of potash, a basic principle of virtually all the later photo-mechanical processes.

### Notary, Julian (1498-1520)

A great English binder, and the last fifteenth-century printer at Westminster, he published in 1518 at London his best known book, the <u>Shepherdes</u> <u>Calendar</u>.

### Nuthead, William

In 1685 he set up his press at Saint Mary's City, the first in Maryland. When he died in 1695 he was succeeded by his widow, Dinah, the first woman in America to be in complete charge of a printing office.

### Nycolson

In 1537 he printed in folio at Southwark Coverdale's second English Bible, the first complete English Bible ever printed in England.

# O

**Oeglin, Erhart (fl. 1507-1512)**
A printer of Reutlingen, he introduced Petrucci's system into Germany. In 1507-1508 he invented music type, cast in copper, for printing in one impression.

**Oswen, John**
An important sixteenth-century Ipswich printer. In 1548 he printed for Grafton the first authorized version of The Book of Common Prayer.

**Otto**
A publisher-bookseller who in 1516 started a business in Nuremberg and became the first publisher-bookseller to purchase manuscripts from authors and to employ printers to produce them.

# P

**Pablos, Juan**
The earliest press to be set up anywhere on the American continent was that of Juan Pablos in Mexico City in 1539.

**Padeloup, Antoine Michel**
One of the most individualistic binders, noted for his forwarding and for his carefully executed decorative bindings in fine leather. He was the successor from 1733 to 1758 to the French Royal Binder Luc-Antoine Boyet, the originator of dentelle tooling.

**Paderborn, Johann**
Also known as John of Westphalia, he introduced printing at present-day Belgium in 1473.

Palmart

He set up the first Spanish press at Valencia in 1474; in the same year apparently he produced the first printed book in Spanish, Fenollar's Obres e Trobes.

Panzer, Georg Wolfgang

One of the first bibliographers of incunabula to excite an interest in early printed books which was definitely typographical. He gathered the titles of all incunabula known in his time in his work entitled Annales typographici (1793-1803) and arranged them chronologically under the names of the towns in which they were printed.

Paravisinus, Dionysius

In 1476 he printed at Milan an edition of the Epitomé, a grammar by Constantinus Lascaris, the earliest book entirely in Greek which was dated and signed by its printer.

Parker, Matthew (1504-1575)

In 1572 he had Day print the De Antiquitate Britannicae Ecclesiae, the first privately printed book which was produced in England.

Parks, William

The first really successful printer to appear in Maryland. Beginning in 1726 he printed at Annapolis for ten or eleven years. In 1730 he set up a press at Williamsburg, Virginia, and became the first printer to actually operate a press there. One of the first items printed at Williamsburg was a sixteen-page pamphlet containing "Typographia. An Ode, on Printing."

Payne, Roger

A peerless eighteenth-century binder, he generally sewed his books with silk thread and used deep purple colored endpapers. It is claimed by some that he invented the practice of damping and rolling morocco in order to give it a straight grain; it is generally agreed that he was the first to create individual binding designs which were appropriate to the spirit of the books.

Peignot, Charles

In 1927 he began the publication of Arts et Metiers Graphiques, a brilliant periodical which was created to stimulate the book arts.

**Pelliot, Paul (1878-1945)**
A noted Orientalist, in 1928 he discovered the earliest dated rubbing which was taken from a stone inscription made by Liu Kung-ch'uan (653-654).

**Peter the Great**
In 1703 he instituted the first Russian newspaper, The News, filling the position of editor himself, which he did by clipping items from foreign newspapers.

**Petrucci, Ottaviano dei (1466-1539)**
He is generally regarded as the father of type music printing. In 1501 he issued at Venice the Harmonice Musices Odhecaton A, which contains the first entirely satisfactory music printing from movable type.

**Pfister, Albrecht**
The first known printer of Bamberg and the first printer to introduce woodcut illustrations. His earliest work was probably Complaint of the Widower against Death, undated, but probably printed in 1460. In 1461 he printed Boner's Edelstein in German, the first book printed in any other language than Latin and the first dated book printed from type with woodcut illustrations.

**Pickering, William**
A nineteenth-century English publisher who in 1829 formed an active association with Charles Whittingham the Younger, a printer. Among the fine editions published by Pickering were the works of Coleridge, various editions of the Prayer Book, and a series of English Poets in fifty-three volumes. In 1844 Pickering and Whittingham printed The Diary of Lady Willoughby in which they employed Caslon's Old Face type, a fact which contributed significantly to the revival of the type, an important event in the history of English typography.

**Pictor**
In 1476 he produced with Ratdolt and Löslein, an edition of the Calendarium, the earliest book with a printed decoration on the title page, specifying date, place, and the names of the makers of the book--hence the first complete title page.

**Pigouchet, Pierre**
In 1491 he produced the Livres Heures, regarded as the finest edition of the work ever published.

Pious XI, Pope
   He affected a remarkable reorganization of the Vatican Library,
   making it one of the most accessible literary institutions in
   Europe.

Pi-Sheng
   Between 1041 and 1049 he invented movable type in China. The
   process was little used, however, because of the lack of suitable
   ink and the inadequacy of the type itself.

Plannck
   In 1497 he printed at Rome the Mirabilia Romae, the first
   guide book.

Plantin, Christophe
   The greatest of all the printers at Antwerp in the sixteenth
   century. He printed many fine books, including the works of
   Virgil (1564), Juvenal (1565), and Ovid (1565); but his most
   famous work was the Polyglot Bible, printed between 1568
   and 1573 and containing parallel texts in Greek, Latin, Hebrew,
   and Chaldean.

Poitevin, Prosper (1810?-1884)
   In 1855 he took out the first English patents in colloid photo-
   mechanics.

Pollio, Asinius
   He founded the first public library in 39 B.C., with the scholar
   Varro as librarian.

Poole, William Frederick (1821-1879)
   The originator of Index of Periodical Literature, 1848--, he
   and Jewett called a conference of eighty librarians at New York
   City in 1853 from which associations of far-reaching significance to bibliography were made.

Portal, Henri
   A seventeenth-century French refugee who, after a short time,
   leased a paper mill near Southampton and in 1713 or 1714 the
   Bere Mill at Whitchurch, Hampshire. In 1725 he was granted
   the privilege of supplying the paper for the printing of Bank of
   England notes, a privilege which is still held by his firm today.

Portilia
    The first printer at Parma, he began to work there in 1472.

Powell, Humphrey (fl. 1548-1556)
    In 1551 he printed at Dublin, Ireland, the Prayer Book of Edward
    VI, said to be the first work printed in Ireland.

Pre, du
    He established the first press at Chartres in 1482-1483 and
    the first presses at three other cities.

Preissig
    In 1909 he brought out the Colored Etching and the Colored
    Engraving, the first important aesthetic treatise.

Pynson, Richard
    A royal printer of the early sixteenth century (to Henry VIII)
    and doubtless the finest printer of his day in England. In 1509
    he introduced roman type into England, using it for the first
    time in the Sermo Fratris Hieronymi de Ferraria. In addition
    to his work as royal printer he found time to print worthy books
    in all classes of literature.

# Q

Quentell, Heinrich
    In 1478 he produced at Cologne the Cologne Bible, the most
    celebrated work of the time. The woodcut illustrations in it
    served as models for many later illustrators.

# R

Ratdolt, Erhard
The greatest Augsburg printer of the fifteenth century. His first
printed work at Augsburg was the Obsequiale; this contained the
first woodcut illustration in colors.

Raverat, Gwendolen
One of two main pioneers of direct-wood engraving of the early
twentieth century.

Reaumur, René Antoine Ferchault de (1683-1757)
He was first to suggest the use of wood as papermaking material
when, in 1719, he had observed the nest making of wasps.

Ricardo, Antonio
In 1584 he set up the first press at Lima, Peru.

Richarde, Thomas
In 1525 a monastic press was established at Tavistock. The
printer was Thomas Richarde, a monk of the monastery.

Richardson, Samuel
An eighteenth-century novelist who, a printer by trade, printed
his famous novels at his own London press.

Ricketts, Charles
In 1896 he established the Vale Press, known for unusual decorative initials and borders designed by Ricketts and for the
integral beauty of the book as a whole.

Robert, Nicholas-Louis
In 1798 he patented a papermaking machine, based on the
principle of an endless wire mesh on to which the pulp flows.
The process was later introduced into England by Henry
Fourdrinier, after whom the machine has been named.

Roger I of Sicily
In 1102 he drew up a deed which is now regarded as the oldest
recorded European document on paper.

Rogers, Bruce
> One of America's foremost type and book designers. As a member of the staff of the Riverside Press, he designed over one hundred special Riverside Press editions. For one of these, a three-volume Essays of Montaigne (1902-1904), he designed a special 16-point face, known as the Montaigne type; for another, an edition of Maurice de Guerin's Centaur (1915), he designed his most popular type, the Centaur type.

Rood, Theodoric
> He introduced printing at Oxford in 1478.

Rooke, Noel
> One of two main pioneers in the modern revival of wood engraving. As a teacher of book illustration at the Central School of Arts and Crafts, and later head of the Department of Book Production, he introduced wood engraving to several artists who later became noted for their art.

Rotherham, Thomas
> He is regarded as the principal benefactor of the Cambridge University Library, the person who probably has more right than anyone else to be called the founder of the library.

Rouge, Le
> In 1487 he was made the first Royal Printer in France.

Rouge, Vicomte Emmanueal de (1811-1872)
> French Egyptologist; discoverer of prototypes of Semitic alphabet in early Egyptian hieratic.

Rubel, Ira W.
> An American lithographer who in 1903-1904 discovered the photo-litho offset method.

Rusch, Adolf
> A probable associate of Johann Mentelin, the first printer at Strassburg (1458), notable for his use of a curiously shaped capital R, in lieu of his name, which caused him to be known to bibliographers as the R Printer. In 1480 he printed a four-volume Latin Bible and in the same year the first practical medical dictionary, De Dondis' Aggregator Paduanus de Medicinis.

Ryland, W. W. (1732-1783)
Engraver to George III, he probably introduced stipple into England, the only country in which the process flourished.

# S

Sanby, Paul
His experiments in the aquatint process resulted in the discovery of a new method of laying an aquatint ground, from which the present name of the process derives.

Savage, William (1770-1843)
He carried out various experiments in color printing, using inks made of balsam capivi and dried turpentine soap.

Say, William
He introduced the use of steel plates, instead of copperplates, for mezzotint work (1820-1821).

Scheele, Karl Wilhelm (1742-1786)
Discoverer of chlorine, he invented the process of bleaching rags for papermaking in 1774.

Schoeffer, Johann
The son of Peter Schoeffer, partner of Johann Fust. His statement, in an epilogue to the works of Livy, that the art of printing was invented by Gutenberg, is regarded as important evidence.

Schoeffer, Peter
When Fust took possession of the Gutenberg plant and equipment, he also took over Schoeffer's services. The first publication of Fust and Schoeffer was a Psalter, dated 1457, the first book to contain its date of printing and the names of its printers.

Scolar, Johannes
In 1528 he printed a breviary for the Benedictine monastery of St. Mary; of this work only one copy survives.

Scoloker, Anthony
He introduced printing at Ipswich in 1547 with a work entitled The Just Reckennyge.

Senefelder, Alois (1771-1834)
He discovered the process of lithography in 1798, and between 1800 and 1803 took over several patents to protect it.

Sensenschmidt
In 1470 he and Kefer set up the first press at Nuremberg.

Sherwin, William
He produced the first dated English mezzotint in 1669, a portrait of Charles II.

Short, Thomas
He introduced printing at Connecticut in 1709, printing official documents of the Connecticut colonial government.

Siberch, John (fl. 1521-1522)
One of England's great binders, he introduced printing at Cambridge in 1521 and claimed to be the first printer to use Greek type in England.

Siegen, Ludwig von
He invented the process of mezzotint, completing his first mezzotint in 1642, a portrait of the Landgravine Ameilia Elizabeth, mother of William VI.

Singrenius
In 1524 he made the first attempt to incline capitals for cursive type.

Sinibaldi, Guittoncino de (1270-1336)
He was a scribe to Lorenzo de'Medici and one of the finest calligraphers of the time. His exquisite Book of Hours provided later typographers with one of the best examples of calligraphy.

Smellie, William (1745-1795)

In 1768 he planned and wrote almost entirely the first numbers of the Encyclopedia Britannica, which was printed by A. Bell and Macfarquhar.

Smith, John (1645-1742)

One of the greatest mezzotint engravers of all time, he engraved several hundred plates, the best of which were portraits.

Snell

In 1482 he printed at Odense, Denmark, the first book in northern countries, Caoursin's De Obsidione et Bello Rhodiano. A year later he printed the first book at Stockholm, Dialogus Creaturarum Moralizatus. In 1495 he printed the first book in the Swedish language, Bok of Djafvulsense frästilse.

Solemne, Anthony de

He established the first press at Norwich in 1566, with which he printed several books in Dutch. His only work in English was Certayne Versis Written by Thomas Brooke (1570).

Speyer, John of

The first known printer at Venice (1469). He died in 1470.

Speyer, Wendelin of

Continued printing for about eight years after the death of his brother. He was the first, it is held, to introduce catchwords at the foot of his printed pages.

Spilman, John

Elizabeth's jeweler who in 1589 was granted a monopoly for papermaking, in which he was active and successful for many years. He was knighted by James I in 1605, following a royal visit to the Dartford paper mill.

Spofford, Ainsworth R. (1825-1908)

As librarian he directed the impressive enlargement of the Library of Congress from a departmental library to a real literary institution.

Spooner, Judah Padock

He set up the first press at Westminster, Vermont in 1780.

**Standsby, William**
He was the most active early seventeenth-century printer, publishing books and music in every branch. For his presswork alone he deserves to be ranked among the best printers of his time.

**Stanhope, Charles Mahon, 3rd Earl**
He was the inventor of the first major improvement upon the hand press (1800). The frame of his press was cast as a single piece of iron, rather than made of wood; and the paten was, by virtue of a series of levers, more easily lowered onto the type.

**Starkey, John**
He issued the first book trade catalog (after the Great Fire) in 1668, known as the Term Catalogues from their having been issued four times a year in the middle of the four law terms of Michaelman, Hilary, Easter, and Trinity.

**Stein, Sir Aurel**
In 1907 he discovered in China a mass of documents written on wood, one or two on silk, and nine letters written on paper in the Sogdian script, all of them belonging to a period of not later than 137 A.D.

**Stout, Elihu**
In 1804 he set up the first press in Indiana.

**Strahan, William (1715-1785)**
He printed the first edition of Johnson's Dictionary of the English Language in 1755.

**Stromer, Ulman**
In 1390 he established the first German paper mill at Nuremberg.

**Suigo, Jacobino**
He was the first Piedmontese printer to work in Turin (1484).

**Swan, Joseph**
In 1879 he patented in England a screen ruled in one direction, which was moved during exposure to obtain a cross-ruled effect.

Sweynheym, Conrad
 He and Arnold Pannartz were the first printers in Italy, setting
 up a press in 1465 at the Benedictine monastery of Subiaco. In
 1470 he began to print an atlas, which eight years later was
 printed from copperplates by Buckinck.

# T

Talbot, Fox
 In 1852 he originated the idea of a screen for halftones.

Tate, John
 He established the first English paper mill between 1490-1495
 near Hartford. Wynkyn de Worde's edition of De Proprietatibus
 Rerum was printed upon paper from Tate's mill.

Teyler, Johannes
 The earliest successful exponent of line engraving in color.
 One of his album of color prints, estimated to date from about
 1670, is preserved at the British Museum.

Ther Hoernen
 In 1470 he printed at Cologne Rolewinck's Sermo in Festo
 Praesentationis Beatae Virginis, historically significant because it is the first book with: (1) a dated title page; (2) a
 colophon on a preliminary leaf; (3) numbered leaves.

Thomas, Eben T.
 A copy of the Indian Bible was purchased for him in 1791; it
 is now in the collection of the American Antiquarian Society.

Thou, Jacques Auguste de
 The most famous book collector and patron of binding in France
 during the second half of the sixteenth century, with a personal

collection of over 8,000 volumes. He was appointed Keeper of the Royal Library under Henry IV.

Tischendorf, Constantine
A well known editor of the Greek Testament, who in 1844 found at Mt. Sinai the Codex Sinaiticus. In 1933 the British Museum purchased it from Russia for $510,000.

Titcomb, Benjamin
In 1785 he set up the first press at Maine.

Tonson, Jacob
One of the most notable publisher-booksellers of the second half of the seventeenth century; the first independent publisher on a grand scale in England; first publisher of Dryden and Pope and the producer of Milton's Paradise Lost.

Torresanus, Andreas
He links together Jenson and Aldus Manutius; upon Jenson's death in 1481 he purchased much of his types and equipment; in 1499 or 1500 Aldus Manutius married his daughter and, in 1507, the two businesses became one.

Tory, Geoffroy
One of the most influential printers in France in the sixteenth century and a master of wood engraving. In 1530 he was appointed printer to François I.

Tottel, Richard
A printer of considerable private means, he was Master of the Stationers' Company in 1579 and 1584. In 1557 he published his Miscellany, the first poetic anthology in England; in the same year he issued Surrey's translation of the Aeneid, the earliest known English blank verse.

Trechsel
He was the first printer in France (1493) to obtain royal protection of a publication. In 1498 he printed his celebrated edition of Terrence at Lyons.

Tritheim, Johannes, real name Heidenberg (1462-1516)
A pioneer bibliographer, his De Scriptoribus Ecclesiasticis, the first great reference work on medieval authors, was printed by Amerbach in 1494.

Ts'ai Lun (50?-118 A.D.)
In 105 A.D. he reported the making of paper from tree bark, old rags, and fish nets. Some even claim for him the invention of papermaking.

Turner, J. M. W.
His major contribution to the art of mezzotint was the application to mezzotint work of landscape studies. Some of his etchings are considered to be among the finest examples of landscape etching ever produced.

Turrecremata, Johannes de (1388-1468)
His Meditationes, the first illustrated book printed in Italy, was published in 1467.

# U

Updike, Daniel Berkeley (1860-1941)
In 1893 he founded the Merrymount Press at Boston, an important influence against affected typography. During the years 1911-1916 he gave the first courses in America on typographical history. These became the basis later for his treatise Printing Types: Their History, Forms, and Use.

Urban V, Pope
He was the first pope to throw the Avignon Library open to students other than the high clergy.

Usher, Hezekiah
He was the earliest bookseller in British North America.

# V

Valdarfer, Christoph (?-1488)
    In 1471 he produced at Florence the first printed edition of
Boccaccio's <u>Decameron</u>.

Van der May
    He made experiments with stereotype plates in 1705.

Van der Meer
    He and Yemantszoen printed in 1477 the first book in Dutch,
an Old Testament without the Psalms.

Van Ghemen
    The first printer of Copenhagen, in 1495 he printed the first
book in Danish, <u>Rijm-Kronicke</u>.

Van Krimpen
    In 1925 the Enschede foundry at Haarlem issued his Lutetia
types.

Vautrollier, Thomas (?-1587)
    In 1570 he published, in an engraved edition, <u>A Booke containing
divers sortes of hands</u> (by De Beauchesne and Baildon), the first
manual of calligraphy to appear in English.

Veldener, John (fl. 1473-1484)
    The first printer of Louvain, and one of the most distinguished
Netherlands printers in the fifteenth century.

Verard, Antoine
    An outstanding fifteenth-century French printer and publisher.
From 1493 onwards he specialized in costly and elaborately
decorated works, usually printed in vellum. He is credited
with almost three hundred publications.

Verovio
    In 1586 he printed at Rome the <u>Diletto Spirituale,</u> containing
the first music from engraved copperplates.

**Vico, Enea**

A sixteenth-century Venetian printer whose books created a vogue for title pages with copper engraved borders.

**Virgil, Polydore**

His History of Inventions, published in 1524, contains a reference to Johann Gutenberg as the inventor of the art of printing.

**Vitré, Antoine (c.1595-1674)**

A distinguished seventeenth-century printer and a favorite of Richelieu, in 1645 he printed the great Paris polyglot Bible in ten hugh folio volumes.

**Von Olpe**

In 1494 he printed Brant's Ship of Fools, one of the most popular and most pirated picture books of the time, and one of the first to deal with contemporary people and their doings, instead of with past personages of heroic stature.

**Von Siegen**

In 1640 he invented the mezzotint process, a method later perfected by Blooteling.

# W

**Walker, Emery**

He and Thomas James Cobden-Sanderson founded the Doves Press in 1900 at Terrace, Hammersmith. Walker was instrumental in the founding of several private presses. In 1931 he was knighted by George V.

**Walpole, Sir Horace**

In 1757 he founded the Strawberry Hill Press.

Walsh, John (?-1766)
>He is reported to have produced the earliest music printing from punched pewter plates in 1720.

Walter, John (1739-1812)
>He established the London Times in 1785 under the name of Daily Universal Ledger.

Wang Cheng
>He is said to have made wooden types in 1314, cutting the characters on a block of wood and then sawing them apart.

Warde, Mrs. Beatrice
>She discovered in the Mazarin Library in Paris and reproduced what appeared to be a unique copy of Jannon's own type specimen book.

Watt, Charles
>In 1851 he and Hugh Burgess successfuly produced a form of chemical wood pulp suitable for papermaking.

Webb, George
>He was the first printer in South Carolina (November, 1731).

Wei Tang
>In 400 he made ink from lampblack, the earliest known wood-block printing ink.

Westphalia, John of. See Paderborn, Johann.

Whatman, James
>In 1775 he exported to the Continent for the first time paper which he had manufactured in England, a milestone in the history of English papermaking. In 1793 he erected a paper mill at Maidstone in which he improved the methods of producing a clean white sheet.

Whitchurch, Edward
>A partner of Richard Grafton. Together they shared the printing of six new editions of the Bible in 1540-1541. In 1543 they were granted a Royal License for the printing of service books; in 1545, another for the printing of primers.

Whittaker, John
An eighteenth-century binder who, following in the footsteps of James Edwards of Halifax, discoverer of a new method of ornamenting bindings in calf, applied acid to the leather with a brush or pen (Etruscan bindings).

Whittingham, Charles
In 1811 he founded the Chiswick Press, one of the outstanding English presses of the nineteenth century, bearer of the highest standards.

Wilford, John
He issued the first really successful book-trade periodical, the Monthly Catalogue. It included English and foreign books and, starting in March 1723, it lasted until 1730.

Willer, Georg
A bookseller of Augsburg, his catalogue issued in 1564 was the first of its kind.

Wolfe, Reginald
A sixteenth-century typefounder and printer, a contemporary of John Day, and the first printer in England who possessed a large stock of Greek letters.

Worde, Wynkyn de
Caxton's foreman, he continued the business when the first English printer died in 1491.

Wotton, Thomas
The most important collector of books during the reign of Elizabeth. Because he adopted a motto similar to that of Grolier, he is often called "the English Grolier."

Wren
Some claim that he invented the mezzotint process.

Wu Chao-i
He was responsible for the beginning of official printing under governmental direction in China.

Wyclif or Wycliffe, John (1320-1384)
    In 1380 he and his followers began their translation of the
    Latin Bible into Middle English; in 1850 the Wyclif complete
    Bible in his original translation was printed for the first time.

# X

Ximenes, Cardinal
    In 1500 he founded the University of Alcalá. He prepared a
    polyglot edition of the Bible and at the expense of 50,000 ducats
    commissioned Arnold Guillen de Brocar to print it for him.
    Often called the Complutensian Polyglot ("Complutension" being
    the Latin word for Alcalá), it was printed in Latin, Greek,
    and Hebrew.

# Y

Yciar
    His writing book, the first published in Spain, and one of the
    finest ever printed, was brought out at Saragossa in 1548.

# Z

Zaehnsdorf, Joseph (1816-1886)
A Hungarian, he founded an eminent London bookbinding firm in 1842.

Zainer, Gunther
A native of Reutlingen, he set up the first press at Augsburg in about 1468 and was one of the first printers to employ woodcut illustrations. His most notable work was an undated Speculum Humanae Vitae, illustrated with many woodcuts portraying the trades of his day.

Zainer, Johann
A relative of Gunther Zainer, he did his earliest work in about 1472. His De Claribus Mulieribus, published in 1473, was the first printed book to contain a woodcut border.

Zell, Ulrich
He was the first printer at Cologne and perhaps one of Gutenberg's apprentices at Mainz. His first book, an undated edition of Cicero's De Officiis, was one of the first classics ever printed.

Zorg, Anton
One of the printers of Abbot Melchior, founder of an early press in his own monastery. Zorg produced many illustrated books; an illustrated Bible (1477); and the first German translation of the Travels of Mandeville (1481).

Zumarraga, Archbishop
He was the patron of the first press in Mexico (1539).

# Bibliography

Aldis, Harry G. The Printed Book. Cambridge: Cambridge University Press, 1947.

Binns, Norman E. An Introduction to Historical Bibliography. London: Association of Assistant Librarians, 1953.
Brinkley, John. Design for Print. London: The Sylvan Press, 1949.
Bowers, Fredson. Principles of Bibliographical Description. Princeton, New Jersey: Princeton University Press, 1949.
Burton, Margaret. Famous Libraries of the World. London: Grafton and Company, 1937.

Carter, John. A B C for Book Collectors. New York: Alfred A. Knopf, 1960.
Clapperton, R. H. Paper: An Historical Account of Its Making by Hand from the Earliest Times down to the Present Day. Oxford: Shakespeare Head Press, 1934.
Cockerell, Douglas. Bookbinding and the Care of Books. London: Pitman, 1944.
Corrigan, Andrew. A Printer and His World. London: Faber and Faber, 1944.

Davenport, Cyril. The Book: Its History and Development. New York: Peter Smith, 1930.

Esdaile, Arundell. A Student's Manual of Bibliography. New York: Barnes & Noble, Inc., 1954.
-----. National Libraries of the World. London: The Library Association, 1957.

Goudy, Frederic W. Typologia: Studies in Type Design and Type Making. California: California University Press, 1940.
Greenhood, David, and Helen Gentry. Chronology of Books and Printing. New York: The Macmillan Company, 1936.

James, Philip. English Book Illustration, 1800-1900. London: King Penguin Books, 1947.
Jennett, Sean. The Making of Books. London: Faber and Faber, 1941.
-----. Pioneers in Printing. London: Routledge and Kegan Paul Limited, 1958.
Johnson, A. F. Type Designs, Their History and Development. London: Grafton and Company, 1934.
Johnson, Elmer D. A History of Libraries in the Western World. New York and London: The Scarecrow Press, Inc., 1965.

McKerrow, Ronald B. An Introduction to Bibliography for Literary Students. Oxford: Oxford University Press, 1927.
McMurtrie, Douglas C. The Book. New York: Covici-Friede Publishers, 1937.
Maddox, H. H. Paper: Its History, Sources, and Manufacture. London: Pitman, 1945.
Morison, Stanley. Four Centuries of Fine Printing. London: Benn, 1949.

Orcutt, William Dana. The Magic of the Book. Boston: Little, Brown, and Company, 1930.

Pottinger, David. Printers and Printing. Cambridge, Massachusetts: Harvard University Press, 1941.

Ransom, Will. Private Presses and Their Books. New York: Bowker, 1929.

Schneider, Georg. Theory and History of Bibliography. New York: Columbia University Press, 1934.
Simon, Oliver. An Introduction to Typography. London: Faber & Faber, 1945.

Tannenbaum, Samuel A. The Handwriting of the Renaissance. New York: Columbia University Press, 1930.

Updike, Daniel Berkeley. Printing Types: Their History, Forms, and Use. Boston, Massachusetts: Harvard University Press, 1937.

Van Hoesen, Henry Bartlett. Bibliography: Practical, Enumerative, Historical. New York and London: Charles Scribner's Sons, 1929.

Young, J. L. Books from the Manuscript to the Bookseller. London: Pitman, 1947.